RESTAURANT REVIEWS: A.K. CRUMP

PROOFREADING: STEPHANIE G. CRUMP, GEORGIA PETERSON DE MACHUCA

PHOTO CREDITS: PHOTOGRAPHS COURTESY OF TCB-CAFE PUBLISHING, SOUTH BEACH CAFE, THE FRANCISCAN, A. SABELLA'S, KIMPTON HOTELS & RESTAURANTS, THE WAX MUSEUM, CIOPPINO'S, THE CANNERY AT DEL MONTE SQUARE, TRE FRATELLI, THE MANDARIN, MCCORMICK & KULETO'S, PIER MARKET, BUBBA GUMP, SIMCO, PIER 39, THE FERRY BUILDING MARKETPLACE, THE CLIFF HOUSE, 21ST AMENDMENT, BEACH CHALET, HALF MOON BAY BREWERY, NAVIO AT THE RITZ-CARLTON, PASSIONFISH, THE FISH HOPPER, THE CROW'S NEST, OLD FISHERMAN'S GROTTO, LOUIE LINGUINI'S, SHADOWBROOK, CARLA CONDON, SKYY VODKA, GHIRARDELLI CHOCOLATE AND TORANI SYRUP, S.N.JACOBSON, BEN SWIRE,

ANY PHOTOGRAPHS NOT CREDITED HERE ARE CREDITED ON THE PAGE WHERE THEY APPEAR. ALL COPYRIGHTS TO PHOTOGRAPHS REMAIN WITH THE PHOTOGRAPHERS OR RIGHTFUL OWNERS.

OTHER PHOTO CREDITS: MONTEREY BAY CONVENTION & VISITORS BUREAU, MONTEREY BAY AQUARIUM (KEVIN CANDLAND, KEN BACH, RICK BROWNE, RANDY WILDER) SAN FRANCISCO CONVENTION & VISITORS BUREAU.

PRINTING: CS GRAPHICS, SINGAPORE

MANY THANKS ARE DUE TO RODNEY FONG AND THE FISHERMAN'S WHARF MERCHANTS ASSOCIATION, AS WELL AS TO ALL OF THE RESTAURANTS AND RESTAURANT OWNERS WHO CONTRIBUTED RECIPES AND OTHER GUIDANCE TO THIS BOOK.

tcb-cafe publishing
PO Box 471706
SAN FRANCISCO, CALIFORNIA 94147
USA

COPYRIGHT © 2005, **tcb-cafe publishing**

ISBN 0-9674898-9-X

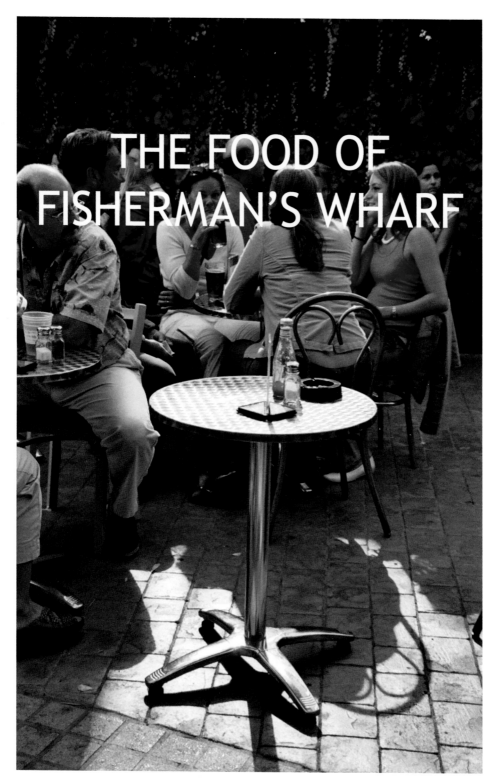

THE FOOD OF
FISHERMAN'S WHARF

Contents

Outdoor Fish Markets
Fisherman's Wharf, San Francisco   Zan 275

Fisherman's Wharf —
A bit of Naples in San Francisco

Above: Historic postcards courtesy of Carol Brockfield

San Francisco is not a large city. It is
barely seven miles on each side, and the population has never reached past one million, even during World War II when there were military personnel stationed throughout. The impact of each of its neighborhoods therefore is that much greater, and the diversity of those neighborhoods is more keenly felt.

Fisherman's Wharf is not only a historic part of San Francisco, but has been at many times the heart of the city. The entire waterfront linked the residents and business owners with their brethren across the Bay to the East, as well as to exotic ports of call in Shanghai, Hawaii, Japan, Europe and South America. Imports of cocoa beans, coffee, tea, and other merchandise formed the lifeblood of several well-known San Francisco enterprises. In addition to these goods were fish, caught daily by immigrants from the Old World, Asia, and the American South, many restarting their lives in Northern California and drawn by the lure of either gold or a fresh start. Times have not always been easy for them, as San Francisco's infamous Barbary Coast reputation illustrates. Through fire and earthquakes, strikes and strike breakers, war and peace, the citizens of the Bay Area have existed and grown.

The most noticeable regional trait emerging from this cornucopia of cultures, businesses, history, lifestyles and language is a true appreciation for good food. In a hard life, the flavors and textures of your meal are often what take you from one day to the next. In San Francisco this was especially true, and visitors today can almost taste the experiences of those early pioneers in the incredible dishes now enjoyed on Fisherman's Wharfs throughout Northern California. From the Portuguese sailors of Half Moon Bay down to the canneries of Monterey, the evolving culinary pleasures of our seaward facing culture are legion.

In this book we seek to capture a bit of that essence, direct you to some of the places in which it can be enjoyed, and allow you to take fond memories back home, whether home is in Northern California or points beyond.

A. K. Crump, Publisher

Fisherman's Wharf is the United Nations of cooking--with everyone bringing something exotic to the table. It's not surprising with its unique blend of cultures and foods that San Francisco has attracted so many creative chefs. When I first arrived, I was immediately drawn to the water-front, the open market, and the awesome collection of fresh fish, vegetables, and fruits. Having grown up around the world--in West Africa, England, Russia and the United States--I felt as though I had finally arrived. It was beautiful but also liberating. From this vantage, I have been able to evaluate flavors and foods from disparate regions and to invent new variations based upon new ingredients. If there is a key to Fisherman's Wharf cooking, it would be to "keep it simple, keep it healthy and keep it fresh." Everyone should eat what they like and remember when cooking to allow all that natural California goodness to shine through each meal and every dish.

Chef Blyden, the 21st Amendment

Above: Historic postcards courtesy of Carol Brockfield

San Francisco is no exception to the rule that there is something distinctive about every city that is a city. With its gay bohemian life, excellent cafes, bright lights and real people, San Francisco is known in every corner of the United States and most parts of the world for its distinctive way of doing things, and particularly its way of enjoying life.

15 January 1919
San Francisco Chronicle

San Francisco

Stalls of Fisherman's Wharf

Clockwise from top left (opposite page): Guardino's seafood cocktails and crab, Fresh cooked crab, Cool storage for fish filets, Fish Grotto #3 and Sabella & LaTorre's restaurant - open since 1927

Alioto's

#8 Fisherman's Wharf   San Francisco   415-673-0183

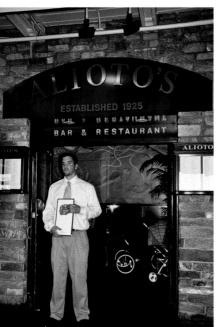

Along with a handful of other Italian immigrant families, the Alioto's 'made' Fisherman's Wharf. If you don't know this then you don't realize why people keep saying, "When you're on the Wharf go to Alioto's." The place is San Francisco history with a dash of parmesan.

Started in 1925 by patriarch Nunzio Sr., the establishment was little more than a fish stand, but evolution from stand to seafood bar was only a short time. Nunzio passed away in 1933, but his widow, "Nonna" Rose, and their children carried on. The rest, as they say, was history.

Alioto's has grown in leaps and bounds, and during World War II became a sailors' favorite for clam chowder, cioppino (seafood stew), steaks, fish, pasta and fresh Dungeness Crab. When the war ended the fame stayed, and now Alioto's classic and contemporary dishes like griddle fried calamari & shrimp, swordfish clubs, octopus & conch salads, artichoke & arugula salads, seafood cannelloni, pan roasted halibut with truffle oil, shitaki mushrooms & pearl onions on a bed of mashed potatoes, and Veal Piccata reign over Fisherman's Wharf.

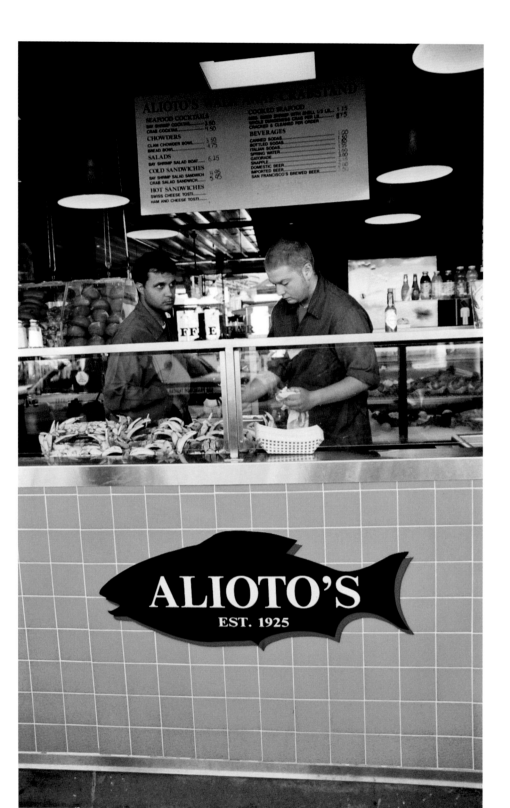

Nonna Rose

#7 Fisherman's Wharf   San Francisco   415-359-1200

When clan patriarch Nunzio Sr. passed away in 1933, the San Francisco food dynasty that would be the Alioto family was left in the care of his widow, "Nonna" Rose. This strong and determined woman did not fail, and her vision has helped make Fisherman's Wharf the cultural and culinary cathedral that we enjoy today.

The quiet little restaurant known as Nonna Rose is a testament to the real woman's work, prowess and taste. Though the space at first glance seems a bit petite, it turns out that the size is actually rather well proportioned. You will find that any number of dining companions can sit together as easily as a table for two can find romantic privacy.

The views of boats in the adjacent marina are intimate and impressive, and the service is equally memorable. Dark woods, deep reds, gleaming chrome and frosted glass are key elements of the restaurant's design, and they produce the feeling of visiting a very connected aunt who totes you to her private dining retreat. There she invites you to chose from a selection of fettucine with bay shrimp, chicken parmesan served with spaghettini pasta, steak & lobster, roasted cracked crab, griddle fried sand dabs, spicy chicken wings, tiramisu or white chocolate cheese cake. Since your aunt lives in San Francisco, she makes sure you accompany everything with a glass of wine, and finish the meal with a cappuccino, espresso, latte.

When I was a little girl, my family had a friend in North Beach named Rose Alioto. She was amazingly rich, and bought a brand-new pink Cadillac every year. I heard this from a lot of people, although not from Rose: she went to Mass every Sunday at St. Peter and Paul's on Washington Square, where a phalanx of impoverished old ladies waited to pay their respects. She would greet each of them, shaking their hands warmly, and slip them some cash.... Rose owned #8 on the Wharf.

She lived on Telegraph Hill in the days when it was a dusty hillside, unlike small hill towns in Italy, and it was populated largely with Italian seamen, who could see when the boats were coming or going from their aerie. The hill wasn't wired for utilities, and cooking was done on open fires in the front of the house.

Rose was a widowed mother of five, and to make money to support the family, she sold some of the food she made to her neighbors. Rose was a wonderful cook, and the smell of her dinners brought hungry seamen from all over the hill. She made money enough to support the family, and finally she rented a small shack on the wharf, where there were no building codes, licenses or any of the other things that make owning a restaurant such an expensive proposition. The Wharf still functioned entirely as a port for fishermen, who brought their catch to her back door, and dined in her place... And the rest is history.

(Alioto's restaurant is now part of a San Francisco culinary dynasty).

P Segal, Founder of Caffe Proust

Above: A view of Fisherman's Wharf from Alioto's restaurant. In front, Boudin Bakery. To left, the Franciscan restaurant.

The Franciscan

Pier 43.5 The Embarcadero   San Francisco   415-362-7733

The Franciscan has been around since 1957, but to a lot of people it seems brand new. That is because in 1997 it undertook a $3 million makeover that completely reconceived the atmosphere and cuisine. Though past customers like Marlon Brando and Mitton Bearle might not recognize the sleek architectural lines, bronze accents and mosaic tiles, they would still appreciate the full Bay and Wharf views.

Franciscan clients now include Sean Penn, Jackie Chan, Danielle Steele and Maya Angelou, who dine on a variety of contemporary Californian dishes. The most popular dish is the cedar plank roasted northern halibut with herbal polenta, but if you're in the mood for dessert you might just go straight to the napolean of summer berries. Over 40% of the clientele is local.

Above: The Franciscan's Melon Soup
Opposite Page: The Franciscan's Ahi tuna, both by Executive Chef Adam R. Jones (photographs courtesy of Chef Jones)

A. Sabella's

2766 Taylor Street, 3rd Floor   San Francisco   415-771-6775

You wouldn't know it by entering this elegant contemporary restaurant with views of the Bay, Alcatraz and the Golden Gate Bridge, but the Sabellas are definitely an "old" San Francisco family. Originally a Sicilian fisherman, the progenitor Luciano immigrated to Fisherman's Wharf in the late 1800's. His rise to culinary fame has been passed from generation to generation. For example, in 1920 Luciano and son Antone open Stall # 3 on Fisherman's Wharf, and in 1940 the A. Sabella family sold Stall # 3 to relatives and the business moved across the street to the old fruit cannery building. A restaurant that was opened in 1954 was destroyed in 1964 by an event that was among the top 10 largest fires in San Francisco. Water was pumped from the San Francisco Bay. It was a full house that night, but everyone left the building calmly and there were no injuries. In the true San Francisco spirit, Lucien Sabella rebuilt the restaurant and was ready for business again in 1967.

During all this time A. Sabella's has entertained "la dolce vita." Legends like Rocky Marciano, Paul Newman, James Brown, Julia Child, Abbott & Costello, sumo wrestlers and football players, even the Sultan of Brunei, have shared their compliments about A. Sabella's garlic roasted crabs, steaks, and cups of molten chocolate.

The staff is also very nice to look at... La Dolce Vita indeed!

Cafe Pescatore

2455 Mason Street   San Francisco   415-561-1111

If you love seafood à la Northern Italy, Cafe Pescatore is not to be missed. Picture the following: Glass of Chianti in hand you admire passersby. The crab ravioli (ravioli con granchio) melts in your mouth. You don't rush, no hurry and no worries, but you also can't quite wait to get to dessert - a Tiramisu with chocolate and toasted hazelnuts. Fellow diners Robin Williams and Carlos Santana give a friendly wave, and you try to remember if you don't have to go to work next week. Instead, you sip more wine... pio desiderio! (wishful thinking).

The variety of culinary choices at Cafe Pescatore is quite large. Notable additions are the zuppa di pomodoro con polenta, a slow roasted tomato soup with creamy polenta and parmesan; pollo al marsala, made of seared chicken breast, garlic whipped potatoes, baby spinach, and a mushroom-marsala sauce; and for those who don't want to get too fancy, pizza rustica, topped with spicy Italian sausage, mushrooms, peppers, marinara sauce and mozzarella. If you're leaning towards a more definitive experience, try either the risotto alla genovese, with bay scallops, sweet corn, sundried tomatoes, basil pesto and parmesan, or the farfalle con pollo, featuring sautéed diced chicken, roasted garlic, sundried tomatoes, pistachios in an herb-white wine sauce.

Artists at Work

The Wax Museum

145 Jefferson Street   San Francisco   800-439-4305

The Wax Museum does not serve food, wax or otherwise, and after seeing some of the scarier exhibits you may not have much of an appetite. On the other hand, seeing lifelike replicas of celebrities such as Keanu Reeves, Madonna, Mike Myers, Nicole Kidman, Angelina Jolie, Ricky Martin, Lance Armstrong, Leonardo DiCaprio and Brittany Spears may build up quite a thirst.

Jefferson Street

Clockwise from top left (opposite page): Franceschi's, Friendly horse drawn carriage, Pompei's Grotto established in 1946, the Anchorage open-air shopping center

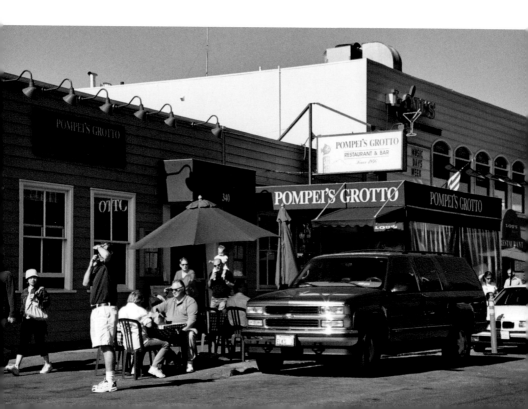

Above: Antique steamboat wheel at the Hyde Street Pier

Cioppino's

400 Jefferson Street   San Francisco   415-775-9311

As you stand in the entrance of Cioppino's, you get a fairly clear idea of the tone they are trying to convey. That tone, in a word, is "Mediterranean." From the sunny colors of the building's exterior to the floors, bar, and tables inside, what you get is a sense of sea, sun, and shellfish. Of course, these are all Italian-flavored. The restaurant is owned by a group of third generation San Franciscans, who point out that their names are not actually 'Cioppino' (so don't ask to congratulate Mr. or Mrs. Cioppino). Instead the owners say that the restaurant is called Cioppino because the word and the dish are an homage to the Italian fisherman who worked so long on the Wharf, and who helped create this fantastic recipe. According to legend, the term "Cioppino" was an Italian accented version of the expression, "Chip in," in which fisherman were encouraged to contribute ingredients to a communal stew.

Regardless of semantic lore, Cioppino's is a very cleverly created establishment. The highlight of the menu goes without saying, but we'll give you the description anyway: "A seafood extravaganza of Dungeness crab, clams, mussels, snapper calamari, shrimp and tomatoes braised in a fennel scented stew. Served original style with whole crab legs." In addition to the house specialty, Cioppino's also offers items such as fried calamari, Dungeness crab cocktails, skewered prawns, chicken marsala, and seafood risotto with scallops, jumbo prawns and mussels.

The Cannery at Del Monte Square

2801 Leavenworth Street   San Francisco Bay   415-771-3112

Like many cities around the world, San Francisco's waterfront was once very industrial. Built in 1907, Del Monte Square is a perfect example, formerly housing the world's largest peach cannery. The brick building has lasted many years, through earthquakes, storms, changes in tastes and wars. Now it is the charming home to a plethora of shops, restaurants, cafes and clubs, such as Club Jazz Nouveau and the Green Room Comedy Club. The European-style courtyard plays host to visitors and locals alike, who casually sit and enjoy the ambiance, accompanied by a beer or a glass of wine, a crepe, or an ice cream.

Days at the Cannery

Clockwise from top left (opposite page): Dining in the courtyard, Fresh organic fruit, Jack's Bar, Organic Farmer's Market, Citrus selections, Chocolate galore

Blue Mermaid
at the Argonaut Hotel

471 Jefferson Street   San Francisco   415-771-2222

The Blue Mermaid Chowder House & Bar compliments its surroundings, and frankly, the 'surroundings' are very complimentary. Set in the Argonaut Hotel and located in the historic Cannery building, the Blue Mermaid excels in chowder. Not just any old chowder, but Dungeness Crab Chowder & Corn, New England Clam Chowder, Hog Island Oyster and Leek Chowder, and several more. The chowder has even won national awards from locales as far away as the state of Rhode Island, where chowder judging is fierce. Of course, if you want more than chowder, you have several other menu choices, like Fish & chips, a steak or a Crab Louis salad.

The design of the Blue Mermaid is relaxed and rustic in 'my favorite fishing boat' style. That is not surprising, considering the Kimpton Group's Argonaut Hotel where the restaurant is located is relaxed and sleek in a 'my favorite family yacht' style. Both styles are complimentary, tasteful and enticing.

Tre Fratelli

2801 Leavenworth Street   San Francisco   415-474-8240

From the outside Tre Fratelli looks like a nice place to sit, situated in the courtyard of the Cannery at Del Monte Square. The location is fortuitous, because it's a perfect place for foot traffic -- people coming in and going out of the building, or taking a shortcut from one side of Fisherman's Wharf to the other. They see the welcoming patio tables of Tre Fratelli and more often than not decide to take a break, have a nice meal, and enjoy the view.

The surprise of Tre Fratelli comes not from the delicious food, which is exactly as one would expect. The menu serves selections of what they call Italo-California cooking, such as Linguini Carbonara made of pancetta, white wine, parmesan, cream, and garlic; Fettucine (Fettucine Frutti di Mare) with fish, prawns, mussels, clams and calamari; and Grilled skirt steak (Bistecca alla Madonna) served over homemade gnocchi with spring asparagus.

The food is good and that is no surprise, not in this city, where good food is de rigor. The Tre Fratelli surprise is actually the decor. There are two styles, both of which are distinctive and appealing. The first style is architectural, and is composed of the brick arches that form the doorways. They evoke a sentiment of a European villa, church, or inn. You are tempted to walk through those arches to discover what lies beyond. What is just around that corner? Perhaps a secret room, private dining, or in Tre Fratelli's case, a comedy club called the Green Room. San Franciscan's have a deep and informed sense of humor and of the ironic, and the Green Room is one of the many outlets for this passion. In addition to comedy, the Green Room also has live music such as jazz, another local favorite.

The other surprise of Tre Fratelli's decor is the lounge area, where the bar is made not of arches and stone but of a very cosmopolitan zebra wood, glossy and curvaceous. The seating in this area is contemporary and sleek, upholstered in tasteful yet very poignant colors and textures. This is a spot where you might meet friends after work, before dinner, or just to chill.

Scoma's

Pier 47   San Francisco   415-771-4383

Scoma's has received several awards for its great meals, and has been rated as one, if not the, best place for seafood in San Francisco. Though some would argue this fact, in particular Scoma's neighbors on Fisherman's Wharf, one thing that is hard to dispute is their long list of fans from around the world, many of whom stop in San Francisco specifically to go to Scoma's. Located on its own little pier, Scoma's is indeed a destination, and the food does not disappoint. The menu includes a variety of dishes, ranging from what may be considered to be rare, the California red abalone with lemon butter sauce, to the more commonplace, such as fresh oysters on the half shell. It also includes specialties that have

been perfected over Scoma's 40 years, like Lobster Bisque, Caesar Salad with bay shrimp, Seafood Cannelloni (crabmeat & bay shrimp in crepes in tomato sauce with melted provolone), Pasta Fisherman's Style with crabmeat, bay shrimp, onions and mushrooms, and Blackened Pacific Swordfish. These courses, on top of Scoma's VIP service, are what make it a perfect stopover.

Indoors & Outdoors

Clockwise from top left (opposite page): Relaxing at Castagnola's, Outdoor seating at Lou's, the legendary Buena Vista Cafe, the facade of Castagnola's

A few words with the San Francisco Maritime National Park Association

When was the San Francisco Maritime National Park Association founded?
The Association was founded in 1950 as the San Francisco Maritime Museum Association, its primary mission was the operation of a museum in the landmark art deco building in Aquatic Park at the foot of Polk Street. In 1954 the Association acquired the tall ship Balclutha, renovated it and opened it for public tours, thereby expanding the concept of what the maritime museum might become.

What kind of facilities can be visited? Are there any ships?
Several ships, including the USS Pampanito submarine museum & memorial, the 1886 square-rigger Balclutha, the 1895 schooner C.A. Thayer, the 1890 steam ferryboat Eureka, the 1891 scow schooner Alma, the 1907 steam tug Hercules and the 1914 paddlewheel tug Eppleton Hall. We also have the Maritime Store, the Visitors Center in the Argonaut Hotel, the Museum and the Library, plus the Hyde Street Pier.

How many people visit?
More than 110,000 people visit USS Pampanito annually, making her one of the most popular historical naval vessels in the country. Considered one of the world's finest examples of maritime preservation, this submarine has been designated a National Historic Landmark. USS Pampanito also hosts more than 15,000 children and adults for overnight education and encampment programs each year. In 2003, for the Association total recreation visits were counted at 4,004,088.

Ghirardelli Square

900 North Point   San Francisco   415-771-4903

Ghirardelli Square is the showcase location of the Ghirardelli Chocolate Company, incorporated in 1852 and America's longest continuously operating manufacturer of premium chocolate products. From humble origins and a stake in the Bay Area during the 1949 Gold Rush, to a growth in its chocolate business that included imports of over 1000 pounds of cocoa beans in 1866, and 450,000 pounds in 1885, the fame of Ghirardelli Chocolate has spread across the globe.

Ghirardelli's chocolate products are for the everyday chocolate lover as well as for the chocolate connoisseur, coming in flavors like dark chocolate, white chocolate, milk chocolate, mint, eggnog, and truffle. The well known Ghirardelli chocolate squares, hot chocolates, baking chocolate and other items can be found throughout the Bay Area, and are often shipped to stores internationally.

Today's Ghirardelli Square still highlights the best of Ghirardelli chocolate, and includes two cafes in which visitors can sit and order a chocolate concoction that will elicit the release of pleasure opiates (yes, it is a scientific fact that chocolate makes you feel really, really good). In addition to the Ghirardelli cafes, the Square is also home to the Sharper Image, an architectural and interior design bookstore, clothings, gift shops, and some of San Francisco's favorite restaurants.

Corners of the Square

Clockwise from top left (opposite page): A chocolate party, the meeting spot at Fountain Plaza, the Woolen Mill Building, Fountain Plaza

The Mandarin

900 North Point Street   San Francisco   415-673-8812

At a recent Ghirardelli Square Chocolate Festival, the Mandarin created a unique and intriguing contribution: chocolate coconut tofu. We asked the management, "Is this a regular menu item?" The answer was "Not really."

This conversation made us reflect on what it takes to have a Chinese restaurant in business for over 35 years in a landmark location like Ghiradelli Square, surrounded by Italian restaurants, seafood vendors and chocolate shops. The answer, obviously, is creativity.

In addition to the great window views, the wooden statues, the archive quality wall prints, the brick walls, the jade, and the 'oh so spot-on' location, the Mandarin's professional kitchen produces exquisite fare which supplies two elements required by an emperor: quality and creativity.

The results are savory selections like crispy taro-wrapped crab claws, phoenix egg flower soup, chicken mango imperial, black pepper beef, and slow-roasted sea bass.

Here's to another 35 years.

McCormick & Kuleto's

900 North Point Street   San Francisco   415-929-1730

The official title of this Ghirardelli Square landmark is "seafood restaurant," but the fact is that the flank steak sandwich with caramelized onions and blue cheese spread is awesome. This is good to know on the rare occasion that you don't order the unforgettable Dungeness crab cakes with red pepper aioli, or the supremely fresh salmon stuffed with crab, shrimp & brie. It's also good to know if you just came by to admire the elegant curves of the rich wood railing, the meters-high windows with views of 'everything,' or the folks at the bar having red wine and beer. The place is huge, but the layout makes it seem intimate in scale. Not only popular with tourists but also with locals who need an ace up their sleeve for restaurant recommendations.

Hopping around the Square

Clockwise from top left (opposite page): Lori's diner, Patio at Frjtz Fries for crepes, Ghirardelli cafe seating, The Cable Car Canteen

Pier 39

Beach Street & The Embarcadero   San Francisco

In the past, Pier 39 elicited a bit of a carnival image to local residents. In their heads they saw flags, merry-go-rounds, shops selling sunglasses and restaurants filled with tourists. This image stemmed a bit from San Franciscans' fear of the mass marketer. It also arose in part from Pier 39's astonishing success. In the minds of the locals, only a mass market-Disney theme park could reach Pier 39's stature of hosting over 10.5 million visitors each year (which by the way, is over 12 times the size of San Francisco's actual population). Eventually the truth was discovered, and it was that Pier 39, the dream of restaurateur Warren Simmons, was successful because it is has three key elements: good fun, good food, and a good location.

Pier 39 does seem a bit like a carnival because things are always happening. People come and go throughout the 45-acre two-level complex, walking in and out of boutiques, visiting the Aquarium, taking a ferry to parts unknown, or just wandering about chatting. The food is world class, highlighting several of the waterfront's specialties such as crab, prawns, pasta, and fish. The location of course provides obvious benefits. On one side you have a view of the city and the Golden Gate Bridge, bordered by a colony of sea lions who are Pier 39's closest neighbors. On the other side you have a view of the Bay Bridge and the East Bay.

It is hard to believe that in the early 1970's Pier 39 was just a derelict dock of wood full of old refrigerators and junked cars, especially when you look at the dazzling array of stimulation it provides today.

Chic's

Pier 39   San Francisco   415-421-2442

We like Chic's because the name sort of surprises us. When you hear "Chic's" you think of 'chic,' a French word for 'stylish and trendy,' which any American restaurant with 'chic' in its name usually is not. Chic's, however, is very chic, and even jaded New Yorkers and San Franciscan gourmands will argue that place is well done.

Chic's is subtle. Everything is nuanced. The view of boats outside have a Monte Carlo-esque feel, and the booths make you want to do something interesting, like having a meal with the family, proposing, or seducing a date. If your date is a vegetarian, not a problem, like any conscientious SF dining establish-ment Chic's has a special vegetarian menu.

You, on the other hand, are more likely to go prawn-crazy. Chic's serves many dishes, like grilled Mahi-Mahi, a Smoked Salmon BLT, and Gorgonzola Salad. But what Chic's really knows is how to handle prawns: fried prawns, prawns scampi, NY Steak & Prawns, prawn and mussel ravioli, Creole prawns, red chili garlic prawns, and even seared prawn with linguini.

When you think about it, prawns are very chic.

Pier Market

Pier 39   San Francisco   415-989-7437

Pier Market has great views of the San Francisco Bay, Golden Gate Bridge, and the sea lions of the Pier 39 Marina. But what is even more interesting to us are the views the outdoor patio provides for people watching of visitors inside Pier 39. Warm and sheltered from any wind, the patio view is undervalued, to say the least.

If you want to sight see without moving from your chair, this is indeed the spot. Of course, if you also like delicious mesquite grilled fresh seafood accented with a glass of California wine, that just makes it even better.

Chose from several dishes, such as popcorn shrimp, sweet and sour calamari, honey barbequed shrimp, Buffalo Wings, trout, salmon, Ahi tuna, linguini & clams, and New York Steak and Lobster.

Even without a lot of buying and selling, the visual and culinary interaction make it a true marketplace.

Bubba Gump Shrimp

Pier 39   San Francisco   415-781-4867

My mother in law, a doctor of social policy and woman of letters, picked up a favorite saying from the mid-90's movie that inspired this restaurant. The phrase was: "And that's all I have to say about that." Such is the impact of Tom Hank's portrayal of the never say die fictional character, Forrest Gump.

Fortunately, Bubba Gump's culinary specialties are far from fictional. Bubba Gump Shrimp has scrumptious specialties that appeal to food lovers from Coast to Coast, especially those who like Southern style recipes. On the menu are Oreo smoothies, Cajun shrimp, clam chowder, cheese fries, chicken tenders with blue cheese sauce, Bourbon Street Mahi Mahi, Southern fried chicken, baby back ribs, and key lime pie.

Bubba Gump also has a gift shop, where you can buy t-shirts, cookbooks, and other nice souvenirs for the kids. If you get down to Monterey you can also visit the location at 720 Cannery Row.

We like to compare a restaurant's longevity to its quality, and seeing that Bubba Gump Shrimp is still doing well after almost a decade of business, "that's all we have to say about that."

Strolling down the Pier

C lockwise from top left (opposite page): Chocolate Heaven, Watching Pier entertainers, Looking for pearls at the Pearl Factory, Aquarium of the Bay

Crab House

Pier 39   San Francisco   415-434-CRAB (2722)

The Crab House is cool. This is a definite statement. When you walk up the stairs to reach the entrance, it is difficult to be sure what you will see. Fortunately, after being greeted by a parade of crabs that look like they've been part of an Andy Warhol exhibit, what you do find is a nice bar, a warm atmosphere, bayside views, and a relaxed crowd of visitors enjoying the pleasures of a certain crustacean.

What is so nice is that everyone is really enjoying themselves. Maybe they're having

the mussels, shrimp & crab combo, the dungeness crispy crab cakes, the crab angel hair lasagna, the seared filet mignon, or the crab enchilada. Perhaps they're just eating a roasted chicken breast & mozzarella sandwich. No one however is complaining about the servings, portions, taste or prices. Satisfaction rules. If it did not, all the restaurant management would need to do is pull out what they consider their big guns, also known as the house specialty: "Killer Crabs" - 2 plus pounds of Dungeness Crabs roasted in a secret garlic sauce.

What might they say when it is served? "Be cool."

Dante's Seafood Grill

Pier 39   San Francisco   415-421-5778

On occasion the weather in San Francisco may be a bit cool for dining al fresco, but Dante's has made sure that the temperature is no longer a deterrent. Their heated outdoor deck allows visitors to not only enjoy savory seafood and other dishes, but to do so while gazing at a panorama of the Bay and San Francisco.

Whether you dine inside or out, the atmosphere at Dante's is relaxed and friendly, and welcomes a range of clients, from parents with children to singles on dates.

The menu items at Dante's pass the "it's San Francisco so it must be good test," and include selections like Chicken rigatoni, angel hair pasta & bay shrimp, baby Maine Lobster tails, rock crab and shrimp cakes, teriyaki chicken wings, crispy fried oysters, and crab claw cocktail.

Forbe's Island

PIER 39, M-1   San Francisco   415-951-4900

San Francisco may be a private yacht kind of town, or a "I don't have a yacht at all, kind of town," but it is definitely not a private island kind of town. Not at least until Forbe's Thor Kiddoo created one of his own. The 50-foot wide by 100-foot long island is actually a type of houseboat, but it is surrounded by approximately 120 tons of rock, 100 tons of sand for a beach, and 40 tons of topsoil. The topsoil is used for his palm trees, which are overlooked by a 40-foot high lighthouse accessible to visitors.

Of course, San Francisco being San Francisco, a guy coming into town and planting his own little piece of paradise right next to Pier 39 did not seem particularly outrageous, especially if he lets other people share in his fortune. Forbes has done that, and welcomes diners to enjoy a menu that includes wild mushroom ragout, toasted brioche, and soft goat cheese; roasted chicken grand-mere with garlic and thyme jus; filet mignon, potatoes au gratin, truffled burgundy demi-glace; and a ginger vanilla crème brulee.

To reach the Forbes Island requires a five minute trip via water taxi. Go to "H" Dock below the Eagle Café to signal the Forbes Island Tiki Boat Shuttle, the "Island Queen."

Above: A view down Embarcadero street, near Pier 23 looking towards Pier 39

Pier 23

Pier 23 on the Embarcadero   San Francisco   415-362-5125

Pier 23 could be a television or movie set in Studio City or Hollywood. If there is sun shining in San Francisco, this is where it will be found. If you need a reminder that the City sits on the waterfront, this is where you come. If you want to check out people from all walks of life having a beer and a mixed drink, you need go no further. Pier 23 is like a setting for other things that are happening in your day or in your life. Each element makes the whole seem a bit surreal, and you find yourself contemplating, "why don't I come here every day?" You think about it some more over a grilled tombo tuna sandwich, fried calamari and café nachos.

A friend once told of a day at Pier 23: "During the whole dot-com bust when people were being downsized left and right, my company announced that they were cutting our staff in half. It was a bombshell, everyone was shocked. You know what we did? The whole company, whether you had been laid off or not, went down to Pier 23 at 2:00pm, and drank all afternoon. I'll never forget that day, it was great!"

You can see why: blue skies, cold drinks, nice views, a bit of live salsa, reggae, funk or jazz music, the possibility of a chance encounter, and time to put your worries aside.

Ferry Building Marketplace

One Ferry Building   San Francisco   415-693-0996

San Francisco sits on a peninsula, which is almost the equivalent of being on an island. The only land approach to the City is from the south. Every other direction requires crossing over water. For many decades this water access was only possible via the scores of ferries that made their way across the bay each day. The main arrival point for these vessels was the Ferry Building, situated in the financial and strategic heart of San Francisco. Opened in 1898, the current Ferry Building has been a hub of activity for over a century. Having survived many threats to its existence, such as the opening of the Bay Bridge in 1936, the Golden Gate Bridge in 1937, the arrival of the motorized lifestyle, and the erection of the physically isolating Embarcadero Freeway, the Ferry Building has once again regained a central role in San Francisco. Ironically, this role was assisted by the Loma Prieta Earthquake in 1989, which seriously damaged the freeway and necessitated its removal. Once removed, the freeway no longer blocked pedestrian and visual access to the Ferry Building, and plans were drawn to renovate the facility.

The renovation of the landmark Ferry Building was completed in April 2003, and now not only is it a hub for water traffic, but also a nexus for food lovers from around the world. The 660-foot long building has over 65,000 square foot dedicated to showcasing the highest quality food and wine from the San Francisco Bay Area. Fresh meats and poultry, fish, wines, artisan cheeses, bread, produce, pasta and pastries can be found in the Ferry Building's marketplace area, in essence a spectacular indoor street. Alongside these stores are cafes, restaurants, design shops, and household appliance stores. The new Ferry Building features gourmet names that make foodies drool, including Sur la Table, the Slanted Door, The Gardener, Stonehouse California Olive Oil, Tsar Nicoulai Caviar, Recchiuti Confections, Scharffen Berger Chocolate Maker, Hog Island Oyster Company , Peet's Coffee & Tea, San Francisco Fish Company, and Cowgirl Creamery's Artisan Cheese.

Public Art on the Embarcadero, Bay Bridge in the background, Travel Photography by S.N.Jacobson

Hi Dive

Pier 28-1/2   San Francisco   415-977-0170

A cool little spot that makes you feel like you're 'down on the waterfront' and still enjoying some modern film noir pizzazz. Hi Dive comes with stylish accent lights, a nice long encapsulating bar, and cool music. Top shelf margaritas are a choice drink, not surprising considering the owner mastered his bar formula and cocktail-culture at his popular San Francisco nightclub/cafe in the SOMA district.

The clientele at Hi Dive is mixed in the truest sense of the word. Some old school dock guys, some new style hipsters, some people who live in the neighborhood and like having a place to go with reasonable prices and a "I've been somewhere" atmosphere.

The food is pretty good too.

Other Bayside Watering Holes for Food, Drink & Music

Below Left: Red's Java House
Below Right: Jelly's, A Dance Cafe

South Beach Cafe

800 Embarcadero   San Francisco   415-974-1115

"They claim we have the best pizza in San Francisco," says owner Michele D'Amico. "It's addictive." High praise indeed, but fortunately well-earned. The South Beach Cafe does have some of the best pizza in San Francisco, though in our opinion it can easily be equaled by the cafe's own chicken with gorgonzola sauce, a dish we often travel well out of our way to sample. The pizza can also be matched by the incredible Italian desserts, several unavailable anywhere else in the Bay Area.

Located on the palm-tree lined streets of the South Beach neighborhood, facing the water and magnificent views of the Bay Bridge and Oakland, the South Beach Cafe feels like you are on vacation even when it's raining. This impression is aided by the decor, a festive, modern look accented by colorful mosaic tabletops of inlaid tile. The music of Italian pop star Eros Ramazatti jams in the background while European soccer plays on the overhead television. Cafe chairs wait outside, providing ample seating for soaking up the rays of the sun and the breeze from the Bay. Newcomers to the South Beach Cafe wonder how they could have ever missed it, and surprised they should be, as it is often the location for many local television shows.

21st Amendment Brewery Restaurant

563 Second Street   San Francisco   415-369-0900

Does anyone remember if the 21st Amendment prohibited the sale of alcohol or permitted it? It doesn't really matter, because here alcohol is more than allowed, it is brewed on the premises. The renovated building and former porn studio was built in 1924, and sits two blocks from the waterfront and the baseball stadium.

The high-ceilinged light-filled dining room is often busy with the after work and lunch crowd, neighborhood types and baseball fans. The food is flavorful and diverse. Favorites are the jerk chicken, hamburgers, and spiced root beer floats. If in San Francisco you ever want a real pork chop or fish & chips then 21st Amendment has it on the menu. The chefs are truly talented.

The Ramp

855 China Basin Street   San Francisco   415-621-2378

San Francisco is like a big solar sun dial. Each hour of the day the illumination is subject to change, especially depending on the neighborhood that you are in. One hour it can be dull and cloudy, the next bright and cheery, the following misty and chilled. If you find that you spend time following the path of the sun across the City, then more often than not you'll eventually find yourself at The Ramp.

Located past the new baseball stadium, the Mission Bay neighborhood and China Basin, The Ramp is not much to look at from a decorative standpoint. For example, the parking lot has storage lockers on either side, filled with who knows what kind of stuff (well, we know at least one has some sort of tool shop inside of it). But once you walk past the front entrance you kind of think to yourself, "I like the big Tiki lounge totem pole over there...those people seem to be enjoying their beers and Bloody Mary's over here...that burger and fries look good right there...that band has a nice Brazilian rhythm to it...and hmmmm, that person over there is kind of cute..."

The Ramp is not all outdoors, there is an indoors section, and at night that has its own unique appeal. But it goes without saying that for San Francisco The Ramp is definitely a sun-day destination.

Kelly's Mission Rock

817 Terry Francois Street   San Francisco   415-626-5355

During the day Kelly's stands out, a large monolithic building by the side of the road, entrance composed of two high gates reaching up to the sky. You wonder, "Is this a restaurant or an airport hanger?" Perhaps it's a fortress, one that requires a special password to enter, or maybe some kind of modern fortress. At night Kelly's becomes even more mysterious, taking on the appearance of a glowing metallic roadhouse. This impression is strengthened by the cars parked outside and the music leaking from the doors, both sure signs that something is definitely going on.

The truth is that Kelly's Mission Rock can best be described as a bastion, an outpost of food, drink, and music in a relatively untouched area of the San Francisco waterfront. You don't really drive past Kelly's by accident, and if so you make a note that you need to return.

Kelly's is a destination, indeed a busy one. At any time of the day something is happening, whether it's brunch, lunch, a wedding reception, a bridal party, a CD launch, or simply a group of friends out cruising while having a bite and a beer. The menu caters to several tastes: gumbo, roast chicken, steak frites, fish & chips, tuna burgers, grilled eggplant and goat cheese, chicken satay, quesadilla, crab omelettes, and even Mom's meatloaf.

The decor is as varied as the menu. There are at least five different areas in which to sit, stand, dance, listen to live bands or just recreate. The building has two levels, both of which include outdoor patio seating, as well as several bars.

San Francisco's Marina District

Eastside West

3154 Fillmore   San Francisco   415-885-4000

Aside from "He looks nice," "She's really hot," "Where are you going this weekend? [Tahoe]" and "Can my kids sit here?" the most common question you will hear at Eastside West is "How are the calamari?" The chorus of answers from everyone around you is always along the lines of "Fantastic!" The fantastic calamari however are just an introduction to the even more fantastic dishes on the menu of this popular Marina neighborhood hangout. Originally promoted as an Oyster Bar, owner Scott Dammann has taken the menu into delicious combinations of American-California-Seafood cuisines. Not to mention that it can all be washed down with a minty mojito or the splendid house cabernet.

Green's

Fort Mason Building A   San Francisco   415-771-6222

To get it out of the way right now, we are going to use the phrase "Green's is a Temple of Culinary Delight." Glad we got that out of the way. It would have been hanging over our heads all the time we described this global destination and original vegetarian Shangri-La, plus the source of revolutionary cookbooks like "Everyday Greens," "Fields of Greens," and "The Greens Cookbook." Green's really put non-meat fare on the map, first because it does it well, and second because it does it with style.

Founded by the San Francisco Zen Center in the late 70's, and located in the renovated buildings of a former military base, Green's is a primal example of how many disparate elements can make a peaceful and enjoyable harmony. The windows bring in light and the movement of water, the walls are tastefully decorated, the staff is pleasant and professional, and the food is world-class. The ingredients are exotic and domestic, recognizable and surprising. Frankly, they can take herbs, tofu, vegetables and spices and create a dish so fascinating that you will want to write home and tell your high school principal.

Here are a few selections from the menu: Linguine with caramelized onions, gorgonzola cream, basil, walnuts, and parmesan cheese; Pizza of spinach and braised endive with sun dried tomatoes, lemon, rosemary, feta, mozzarella, and parmesan cheese; and Marinated and mesquite grilled Tofu with tomatoes, lettuce, mayonnaise, and horseradish on whole wheat bread. Don't forget to select a glass of wine and prepare for dessert. Perhaps a Chocolate Hazelnut Mousse Cake?

After Green's, you might never again ask, "Where's the beef?"

Warming Hut Cafe

Presidio Building 983, Crissy Field   San Francisco   415-561-3042

Located at the bay's edge of the Presidio between the Golden Gate Bridge and the Palace of Fine Arts, Crissy Field has been through many changes over the last century. First it went from shellfish-rich natural wetland to military airstrip, then to barracks-laden military base, then to deserted weed-infested jogging path and

launch pad for windsurfing, and now after several years, much civic activism, and $34 million dollars, it has been restored to a balanced version of its original state. The ecosystem has been reconstituted, the sand has been cleaned, and bikers, runners, kite-flyers, and families with picnics are the new users for this property. Sitting at the Golden Gate Bridge end is the Warming Hut Cafe & Bookstore, an old mine storage building completely converted to modern service using state-of-the-art sustainable practices. The insulation is made of recycled blue jeans, the furniture from salvaged wood, and the cuisine from a variety of organic fair-trade foods inspired by Chez Panisse's star chef, Alice Waters.

The Warming Hut is a good place to stop when out enjoying the day in Crissy Field, at the beach, or on the bridge, but we've found that it is also a good place to go when the day is nice and that's all you need - unless you include one of the most beautiful views in town.

Above: Renovated and spacious Crissy Field, perfect for walks, picnics, kite flying and wind-surfing.

The Beach Chalet

1000 Great Highway   San Francisco   415-386-8439

Nestled at the foot of the continent and overlooking a view that extends to Hawaii and faraway Asia, the Beach Chalet is known for its sunsets. As the sun glides slowly over the horizon and down into the sea, diners and spectators stop what they're doing and gaze at this gift of nature. In this way the Beach Chalet fulfills at least one objective: creating a memorable experience.

The Beach Chalet itself is a standing ode to memory. First opened to the public in 1925 as a bath house and restaurant, the Beach Chalet has endured the vagaries of time. In 1936 its walls were covered with colorful murals, mosaics and wood carvings. The murals that one can see today reflect life as it was at the time. Lucien Labault's frescoes depict San Francisco during the Great Depression, including districts such as the Embarcadero, Fisherman's Wharf, Baker Beach, Golden Gate Park, Land's End, the Marina, Downtown, and Chinatown. Not long thereafter the facility was turned into a barracks for troops. Later in its life the Beach Chalet fell into disrepair, and became a roadhouse and haven for questionable activities. For most of the 1980's it stood unused, until Greg Truppelli and partners opened it as brew pub, restaurant and semi-museum in 1997.

The Beach Chalet menu is "Modern American Cuisine," and features standouts like buttermilk fried calamari, garlic french fries, portobello mushroom melts, fish and chips, pan roasted herbed chicken, garlic mashed potatoes, and housemade butternut squash ravioli with lemon-sage brown butter, goat cheese, walnuts and arugula.

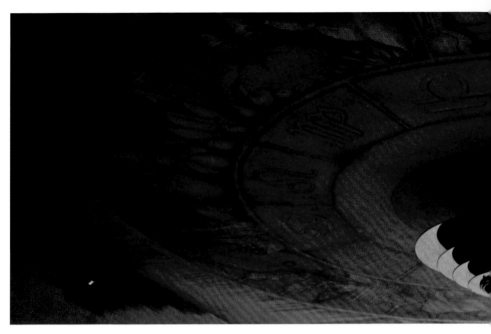

Above: Fresco on the ceiling of the Beach Chalet stairwell. Below: Beach Chalet Visitor's Center

Recreation in
the Park

The Park Chalet

1000 Great Highway   San Francisco   415-386-8439

Opened in the Spring of 2004, the Park Chalet is a newer addition to the historic Beach Chalet restaurant and visitor's center. Whereas the Beach Chalet faces Ocean Beach and the Pacific Ocean, the Park Chalet faces Golden Gate Park. The Park Chalet uses this to its advantage. The floor-to-ceiling glass walls are open to a manicured lawn where children play and friends lounge. On warm days the walls swing open, exposing the entire inside of the restaurant to the weather and making it into an outdoor cafe. Even on cloudier days the light fills the room, making it cozy and inviting, especially when the central fireplace is stoked and the cocktails flow.

The decor of the Park Chalet is modern and slightly abstract, with vivid colors and clean lines dominating the theme. The building itself demonstrates this concept, while simultaneously honoring the landmark architecture of the Beach Chalet. To achieve this symbiotic effect, the same architects who were involved in the Beach Chalet renovation, Heller·Manus, brought their talent to the project.

At night the Park Chalet is like a jewel, and live music is often available. Keeping the serene yet groovy atmosphere, the lineup includes a variety of bands performing Instrumental Surf, Intimate Jazz, Acoustic Blues Jams, San Francisco Soul, and Latin World Beat.

The Cliff House

1090 Point Lobos   San Francisco   415-386-3330

The Cliff House near Ocean Beach began a major renovation project in January 2003. According to the project team, led by C. David Robinson Architects, Brayton + Hughes, and Mark Hulbert of Preservation Architecture: "The original Cliff House was built in 1863 and hosted prominent San Francisco families including the Hearsts, Stanfords and Crockers, as well as three U.S. presidents. After being destroyed by fire, it was rebuilt in the style of a French chateau in 1896 by millionaire and future mayor Adolph Sutro. Following another fire, Sutro's daughter Emma resurrected The Cliff House in a neoclassic design in 1909. That structure remains today as the inner core of the current building, which was acquired in 1977 by the National Park Service." Today's Cliff House Bistro is a modern San Francisco dining establishment with the same stunning views as the original, able to keep one foot in the past while the other is firmly set in the future.

Right: The renovated historic Cliff House, by C. David Robinson Architects. Renderings by Michael Reardon

The Peninsula: Half Moon Bay

Half Moon Bay Brewing Company

390 Capistrano Road   Princeton-by-the-Sea   650-728-BREW(2739)

If you don't live in Half Moon Bay you may not have heard of this spot, and that may be good for the rest of us. We love to jump in the car and head over on a Sunday afternoon for live music, fresh beer, cool wine and a seat on the patio next to the firepit. The crowd is a wild mix of all generations and tastes, and watching attractive 20-somethings hanging out with friends next to 60-year old dancing lotharios just makes you feel good. The oceanfront restaurant is only 1/4 mile from Mavericks, the famous big wave surf spot, which is the namesake of their Mavericks Amber Ale. Of course with visitors like surfer Jeff Clark, Pierce Brosnan, and Backstreet Boy AJ Maclean, this cool hangout can't stay too much of a secret.

BREWERY SPECIALS
w/a BEER!

BROILED SWORDFISH *
ROASTED PRIME RIBS *
MAHI MAHI *
FILET MIGNON *
MAINE LOBSTER *
CEVICHE *
SOUP - SPLIT PEA

ORDER HERE

Above: Inside the Half Moon Bay Brewing Company

Navio at The Ritz-Carlton, Half Moon Bay

One Miramontes Point Road   Half Moon Bay   650-712-7000

Navio means 'ship' in Portuguese, and was named for the Portuguese vessels that first entered Half Moon Bay centuries ago. Located on a high bluff overlooking the Pacific coastline, this modern elegant restaurant is the culinary highlight of the 261-room golf & spa resort that is the Ritz-Carlton, Half Moon Bay. Navio's chef uses the finest locally available ingredients, evident even on the appetizer menu that includes Dungeness crab salad and seared Diver scallops.

A sample of what you might find on the Navio's Lunch Tasting Menu includes chilled smoked trout soup with celery and caviar vinaigrette, Pastorino Farms beets with Harley Farms goat cheese and arugula salad, Wild Troll king salmon escalope with grated yellow corn and roast tomato sauce, and Frog Hollow peach and champagne soup with yogurt sorbet. The wine list that accompanies these selections ranges from a Napa Sauvignon Blanc to a Colchagua Valley Syrah, all chosen by the chef for their complimentary tastes.

The seasonal nature of Navio's offerings even extends to the seductive warm chocolate bread pudding and October's festive seven-course pumpkin tasting menu. Luxe par excellence: Several dining nooks not only have ocean views, but can even be enclosed by drawn curtains for additional privacy. (after the chocolate bread pudding, of course)

Above: The Navio Chef's Table. Opposite Page, Top: Navio's open kitchen. Opposite Page, Bottom: The Ritz-Carlton, Half Moon Bay

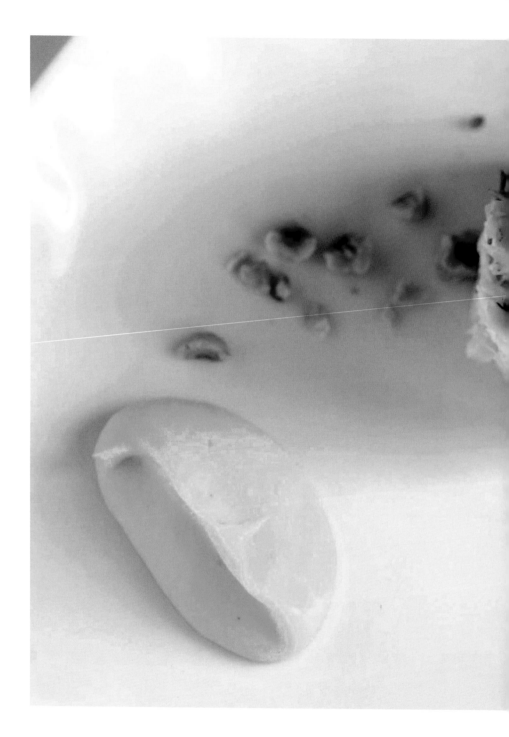

Above: Navio's Hand Picked Dungeness Crab Salad with Roast Acorn Squash, Butternut Puree and Hazelnuts, by Chef Peter Rudolph. All Navio photography courtesy of Navio at The Ritz-Carlton, Half Moon Bay. Photo above taken by photographer Vanessa Gavalya.

Monterey Bay: Santa Cruz and Monterey

Fisherman's Wharf in Monterey is one of the jewels of Northern California. Stunning ocean views, award-winning cuisine, and a family-friendly environment make it a "must visit" destination. Locals and visitors alike enjoy the energy, the smells, and the tastes of Fisherman's Wharf Monterey.

Brenda Roncarati
Monterey Peninsula
Chamber of Commerce

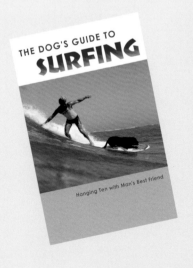

THE DOG'S GUIDE TO
SURFING

Hanging Ten with Man's Best Friend

Passionfish

701 Lighthouse Avenue   Pacific Grove   831-655-3311

'Fine wine for fine meals' could be Passionfish's motto, and it would explain why this restaurant has received Wine Spectator magazine's Award of Excellence. Popular with locals as well as visitors to Pebble Beach, the establishment is a casual 'foodie' haven. Seasonal specials are the Monterey Bay spot prawn with garlic butter or the black pepper and fennel crusted seared Ahi tuna with wasabi slaw. A favorite dessert is the gorgonzola cheesecake.

The proprietors are major advocates of sustainable seafood education and awareness, and are very supportive of local fisherman. The support is bilateral. One night when the halibut ran out a local fisherman zoomed over with buckets filled with flopping fresh fish, greeted by cheers and applause from the customers.

The Fish Hopper

700 Cannery Row   Monterey   831-372-8543

The Fish Hopper is built on a pier extending into Monterey Bay, and has one of the largest outdoor dining patios in town. Every seat offers an excellent view of the water and surf. Another benefit of the view is that at least a dozen times a year you may see Humpbacks breaching -- jumping full out of the water -- only a couple hundred feet from the restaurant's windows (apparently some visitors think it's a scheduled show).

The Fish Hopper describes its menu as "California Cuisine with a Mediterranean Flare!" The Swiss-trained executive chef is very creative and has a regular following. The most popular dish is the fresh Monterey Bay salmon, crusted with sweet Dungeness crab with artichoke hearts and portobella mushroom. There are also a variety of specialty dishes that change seasonally, based solely on fresh seafood and local Salinas greens. This rotating menu is in keeping with the Fish Hopper's adherence to the guidelines of the Monterey Bay Aquarium's Seafood Watch Program, in which restaurants purchase and serve seafood that comes from healthy fish populations, harvested in a manner that does not harm the environment.

The Crow's Nest

2218 East Cliff Drive   Santa Cruz   831-476-4560

Strategically located right on the beach, the Crow's Nest sits at the entrance to the Santa Cruz Harbor. This vantage point offers luxurious views of the entire Monterey Bay. In addition to the regular views, above the restaurant sits a working Coast Guard lookout, a "Crow's Nest." The restaurant's management is very beach, ecological and civic-oriented, in keeping with the Santa Cruz lifestyle. Surfer Robert "Wingnut" Weaver of the surf film "Endless Summer 2" is a former bus boy at the restaurant. His longboard from the film hangs in the upstairs lounge as part of the Crow's Nest classic surfboard collection.

The Crow's Nest serves fresh seafood, specialty pasta dishes and quality steak. Some of the more popular menu items include grilled halibut with a pesto crust served with artichoke risotto, house smoked salmon with wasabi sauce, and the specialty dessert, the Chocolate Bombe.

The clientele is a mix of tourists and locals, as well as families and couples on dates. In the evening singles and couples enjoy the nightlife in the upstairs lounge.

Old Fisherman's Grotto

39 Old Fisherman's Wharf   Monterey   831-375-4604

Old Fisherman's Grotto has stood on Monterey's Old Fisherman's Wharf since the 1950's, when the owner's three fishing boats supplied the daily catch. The boats are now gone, the fish today comes from sustainable seafood sources, and Old Fisherman's Grotto remains a beloved dining fixture in Monterey.

The menu offers seafood, pasta, steaks and vegetarian fare. A house specialty is cioppino (shellfish and fish in a marina sauce broth), and the macadamia nut crusted halibut topped with tropical salsa is a favorite. The clam chowder is also popular, even winning a Reader's Choice Award in 2004. Of course, if you can't get enough chowder at lunch or dinner, you can always take home a special canned version - over a million have already been sold.

Portola Cafe

886 Cannery Row   Monterey   831-648-4870

So, you're having lunch and a whale swims by, what do you do? At the Monterey Bay Aquarium's Portola Cafe every table gets the use of a pair of binoculars and a wildlife spotting guide. This allows you to put down your chocolate bread pudding, pick up the field glasses and try to identify the species. "Gray or humpback?" In between mouthfuls of the Coastal Stockpot (fresh fish & shellfish from sustainable sources in a silky tomato-saffron broth), your partner may make helpful suggestions. Or they may be eyeing your bread pudding while mumbling about dolphins chasing seabirds on the horizon.

The Monterey Bay Aquarium

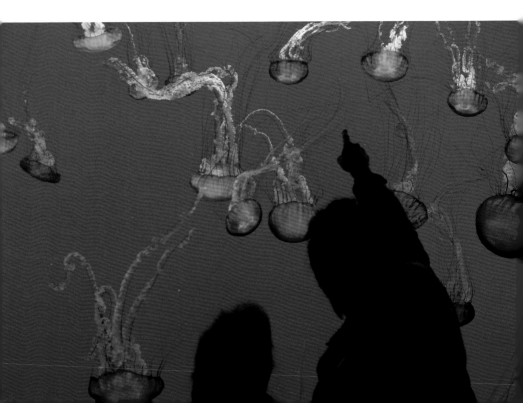

Clockwise from top left (opposite page): Oceanfront decks of the aquarium, Overhead Anchovies exhibit in Outer Bay galleries is a kinetic whirlpool of activity, Toddler activity area in Splash Zone, The Sea nettle exhibit is mesmerizing and soothing

Louie Linguini's Seafood Shack

660 Cannery Row, Second Floor   Monterey   831-648-8500

It is not unusual to wonder if Louie Linguini is actually a real person, unless of course you know him. Born in the Italian seaport town of Portofino in 1930, Louie came to America with his family to avoid the hardships of World War II. Their eventual destination was the little village of Monterey, where his father worked as a sardine fisherman and his mother was employed on Cannery Row. After serving in the U.S. Marines, Louie started his acting

career and appeared in several movies, as well as ran around with the celebrity-filled Rat Pack of Frank Sinatra and Dean Martin. After a long and adventurous career however, in 2004 and at the age of 74 Louie settled down and opened his Monterey-based Italian seafood restaurant. Apparently there were a few things he hadn't gotten around to in his long life, and running a restaurant in his Golden Years was one of them. Our good fortune. Louie shares with us several of his favorite recipes, including fried mushrooms, Dungeness crab salad, shrimp gorgonzola rigatoni, spaghetti & meatballs, lemon caper chicken, a steak & salmon combo, and his Linguini seafood platter with fried popcorn shrimp, clam strips and calamari.

Shadowbrook

1750 Wharf Road   Capitola   831-475-1511

Sitting on Soquel Creek just minutes away from the Pacific Ocean, Shadowbrook has an ambiance that makes you want to be in love. In fact, New Woman magazine once wrote that it was "the most romantic restaurant in the galaxy. People have been known to propose to people there that they don't even like." We don't know anyone so overcome with emotion, but there is no doubt that it has the right vibe.

The food is delicious, and the dessert most on everyone's lips is the Jack Daniel's Mud Pie. We're still trying to find out what Arnold Schwarzenegger said when he ate at Shadowbrook, but you can guess it probably was; "I'll be back."

MONTEREY BAY AQUARIUM®

Seafood
WATCH®

Chinook salmon

West Coast
Seafood Guide

Seafood Watch Program:
Monterey Bay Aquarium

People once thought that ocean fisheries could never be exhausted. They were wrong. As seafood stocks come under increased pressure worldwide, the Monterey Bay Aquarium offers individual consumers, restaurants and retailers a way to preserve the health of ocean wildlife through their seafood choices.

Called "Seafood Watch," the program uses science-based fisheries research to create a consumer pocket guide and other materials that help consumers and suppliers choose seafood from well-managed fisheries - a buying decision that can help assure healthy oceans for future generations.

According to aquarium Executive Director Julie Packard, "Fisheries conservation is among today's most important marine conservation issues. The solution is in people's hands every time they select seafood."
In growing numbers, individuals are using regional "Seafood Watch" pocket guides to make their seafood selections. And restaurants are changing their menus to offer more and more "Best Choices" - seafood that is abundant and caught or farmed in ways that does not harm the ocean environment.

Because information is constantly evolving, the pocket guides are updated twice a year. You can learn more and download a pocket guide at www.seafoodwatch.org.

The North Bay:
Marin County

Tasting Tiburon

Clockwise from top left (top of page): Sweden House Bakery & Cafe has nice water views, Sweden House Bakery & Cafe interior, The Waters Edge hotel, Top deck of the popular Mexican seafood spot Guaymas Restaurante, (bottom of page) Historic downtown Tiburon, Guaymas' attentive staff, Fashionable cafe to see and be seen, Guaymas busy patio

Sam's Anchor Cafe

27 Main Street   Tiburon   415-435-4527

We love Sam's Cafe, that is, when we can get a seat outdoors. Which is about 75% of the time, not a bad average for a place with one of the best views of the Bay, Angel Island, and glorious San Francisco on a sunny day. Going to Sam's is always like a mini-vacation.

Sam's has well prepared food and a good choice of drinks, pleasant service, and choice seats. Of course, it's all about the seats. When you're sitting outside on Sam's deck it is very easy to forget that your chair is literally situated over water, or that San Francisco, which seems so close, is actually 20 minutes away by car.

Birds put things in perspective, as they swoop over the tops of the docked sailboats in the little Tiburon marina in front of the restaurant. If you're one of the fortunate who has your own vessel you can even pull right in for lunch. If you like boats but don't have access to one, then you can still take a ferry from Fisherman's Wharf, then go to Angel Island and build up an appetite with a nice bike excursion.

Inside of the restaurant, Sam's has a tranquil atmosphere, perfect for brunches, romance, family meals, and groups. The food is solid Northern California coastal cuisine: cioppino, steamed clams, oysters, swordfish, salmon, grilled prawns, grilled tofu-vegetable brochette, beer batter onion rings, organic baby spinach salad, and a very long brunch menu.

Above: The interior of Sam's Anchor Cafe in Tiburon

Stepping Through Sausalito

Clockwise from top left (opposite page): On the rocks watching the boats, Friendly pets, A cool ice cream, Historic fountain, prestigious Sausalito Yacht Club, historic square, Sitting by the water, Perusing art galleries & shops

NORTHERN CALIFORNIAN
COASTAL CUISINE

Chance is always powerful. - Let your hook be always cast;

in the pool where you least expect it, there will be a fish.

-- Ovid

Stuffed Striped Bass

San Francisco Fish Company,
Ferry Building, San Francisco

Serves 2

*1 whole striped bass,
scaled, gutted and
butterflied
1/2 bulb fennel
3 green onions
1 stalk of celery
4 mushrooms
1/4 bunch Italian parsley
1/4 cup currants
1/4 cup seasoned bread
crumbs
Beaten egg to moisten*

Clean and chop fennel, celery and green onions into 1/2 inch dice. Place in a small bowl. Chop mushrooms into 1/2 inch dice and place into separate bowl. In a medium sauté pan on medium, heat olive oil and sauté mushrooms, seasoned with salt and pepper until softened. Transfer to bowl to cool. Add more olive oil and sauté remaining vegetables, seasoned with salt and pepper until softened and then add to mushrooms. Stem and chop parsley and add to the cooled vegetables. Add currants and breading to the mixture and combine. Add beaten egg to moisten and bind the mixture.

Take the butterflied striped bass, sprinkle inside cavity with salt and pepper. Pack the cavity with the stuffing. Fold the other side of the fish over the stuffing and secure the stuffing by tying butcher twine around the fish in 1 inch increments. Bake at 375 degrees Fahrenheit for about 30 minutes or barbecue the stuffed striped bass until 145 degrees Fahrenheit in the center with a meat thermometer. The outside of the fish can be coated with olive oil and salt and pepper prior to cooking.

Strudel Of Smoked Salmon, Mascarpone & Asparagus With 40-Year Old Balsamic And Quail Eggs

The Franciscan, San Francisco
Adam R. Jones, Executive Chef

Serves 4

Heat canola oil to 375 degrees Fahrenheit, and set oven to 350 degrees Fahrenheit. In medium sized pot, bring one quart water and 1 Tbs salt to a boil; reduce to a simmer. Cook quail eggs for two minutes; remove and allow to cool for 10 minutes. Peel, cut in half lengthwise, and set aside. Rub asparagus spears with olive oil, salt and pepper; roast in oven for ten minutes, or until barely fork tender. Set aside. Prepare a slurry by mixing the water and rice flour with a fork. Season with salt and pepper. Set aside.

For Strudel: Lay one sheet of egg roll wrap down on work surface, so that a corner faces you; brush with slurry. Lay another piece about 1.5 inches to the left, overlapping the first piece by about five inches. Spoon three oz mascarpone into center, and spread around, leaving a two inch border all around the sides. Next, layer 4 pieces roasted asparagus spears into center of pastry. Continue with 2 oz sliced smoked salmon; sprinkle with salt and pepper. Brush sides with slurry mixture. Roll forward, starting with the part facing you, until you reach about a quarter of the way. Tuck in either side toward the center, and continue rolling away from you (this method is similar to rolling a burrito). The strudel should stick together at seams, and be about 1.5 inches in thickness. Repeat for the other three portions, and set aside. Fry each strudel in heated canola oil for about two minutes (you only want to temper the cheese, be careful not to cook the salmon!) Rest strudels on paper towels while assembling the plates.

To assemble, cut strudel on drastic bias lengthwise; plate with micro arugula. Drizzle the balsamic & truffle oil around sides; place two medium rare-poached quail egg halves around the strudel.

8 sheets of egg roll wrapper
8 oz sliced smoked salmon
12 oz mascarpone cheese
12 spears asparagus
1 oz water, cold
1 oz rice flour (or all purpose flour)
8 quail eggs per serving
4 teaspoons white (Alba) truffle oil
40-year balsamic vinegar, as needed
Pure olive oil, as needed
Kosher salt
Freshly ground black pepper
Canola oil (for frying)
Micro (or baby) arugula for garnish

Dungeness Crab Cakes

McCormick and Kuleto's Seafood Restaurant, San Francisco

"There are as many recipes for crab cakes as there are chefs. This one takes the straightforward approach, whisk we think is best. Try not to break up the crab meat too much while you're mixing. The texture will be better if the crab is chunky."

Makes 8 cakes. 3 1/2" in diameter, or 30-40 mini-cakes for hors d'oeuvres.

1 1/2 Lb crab meat, cleared of shell fragments
1 cup plain bread crumbs
2 celery stalks, finely minced
1 small onion, finely minced
1 small green pepper, finely minced
1 tsp dry mustard
1/2 tsp Tabasco
1 large egg
1/4 cup mayonnaise
1 Tbs Worcestershire sauce
Additional bread crumbs for coating the crab cakes
1/2 cup oil for frying (or more)
1 cup jalapeno hollandaise (see below)

Hollandaise Sauce, Makes about 1 1/2 cup
1/2 Lb unsalted butter, melted and warm, but not hot
3 egg yolks
1 Tbs water
1 Tbs lemon juice
Pinch salt

Hollandaise Sauce: Melt the butter and reserve. Combine the egg yolks and water in the top of a double boiler over hot, but not boiling water and stir briskly with a wire whisk until the mixture is light and fluffy and the consistency of light mayonnaise. Remove the tip of the double boiler from the heat and slowly add the butter in a thin stream, while continuing to whip the mixture. Season the mixture with the lemon juice and salt to taste.

Crab Cakes: Preheat oven to 200 degrees Fahrenheit. Combine all the ingredients except the bread crumbs for coating, the oil for frying and the tartar sauce. Form the mixture into eight 3 inch to 3 1/2 inches by 1 inch thick crab cakes, or 30 to 40 mini-cakes for hors d'oeuvres. Coat cakes on both sides with the additional bread crumbs, patting the crumbs lightly into cakes. If you are making large cakes, put about 1/4 cup oil into a 10" to 12" saute pan and cook over medium heat. Cook 4 cakes at a time, 4 minutes per side. They should be nicely browned on both sides and heated through. Keep the 4 cooked cakes warm in the oven while you prepare the remaining 4. Use fresh oil for the second batch. If you're making mini cakes, put the entire 1/2 cup oil in the saute pan and fry 10 to 15 at a time, turning once until dark brown. You may need to replace the oil once between batches of mini cakes. Keep cooked mini cakes warm in oven while you cook the rest.

Cioppino

Beach Chalet and Park Chalet, San Francisco

Cioppino Sauce: Heat olive oil in large saucepan. Add onion, celery, carrots, and garlic. Cook for 3 minutes, stirring occasionally until vegetables begin to soften. Add the white wine, clam juice, tomato paste and tomatoes. Bring to a boil, reduce to a simmer, cook slowly for 30 minutes. Add all other ingredients, simmer 5 minutes. Remove from the fire and set aside. Salt and pepper to taste. Note: This sauce can be produced a day ahead

Cioppino: In a saute pan, heat the olive oil. Add the clams and mussels, heat for one minute until just beginning to open. Add shrimp, cook briskly for one minute. Add the Cioppino sauce, the Mahi Mahi and Dungeness crab. Cook until just heated through. Add the parsley, toss once, and serve in bowls.

Four generous portions

Cioppino Sauce
2 Tbs pure olive oil,
4 oz diced yellow onions
2 oz diced celery
2 oz diced carrots
1 Tbs chopped garlic
2 cups white wine
2 cups clam juice
2 Tbs tomato paste
32 oz crushed tomatoes
1/4 tsp chili flakes
1/4 tsp ground black pepper
1 tsp saffron
1 tsp thyme, dry
2 Tbs fresh chopped parsley
1 Tbs fresh chopped oregano
1/2 to 1 tsp kosher salt

Cioppino
1 Tbs olive oil
12 each manilla clams
8 each prince Edward island mussels
4 shrimp, peeled and de-veined, 41-51 size (or any shrimp that you prefer)
Cioppino sauce
8 oz of mahi mahi, cut into bite size pieces
2 whole fresh Dungeness crabs, poached, cleaned and cut into quarters
2 Tbs chopped Italian parsley.
Lobster crackers
Sides of lemon
Side of garlic bread

Chocolate Mousse Cake

Forbes Island, San Francisco
Terrance MacDevitt -Chef du Cuisine

Crust: Mix all ingredients in mixing bowl with melted butter. Press into springform pans and let set at least 20 minutes

Mousse: Cream sugar and butter together in mixing bowl. Use whisk and add eggs one at a time. Temper chocolate (melt in double boiler over water). Into melted chocolate add vanilla and cream, whisk until full incorporated. Divide evenly into two chilled springform pans. Chill for 1 hour. Remove from springform pans

Crust
6 oz toasted ground pecans
8 oz toasted ground hazelnuts
8 oz melted butter
1 cup packed brown sugar
A pinch of cinnamon
A pinch of salt

Mousse
40 oz dark chocolate
12 eggs
1 1/2 cups granulated sugar
12 oz softened butter
2 tsp vanilla
1/4 cup cream

Watermelon and Roasted Poblano Chile Salad

Forbes Island, San Francisco
Terrance MacDevitt -Chef du Cuisine

Serves 6

Combine all ingredients in chilled stainless steel bowl. Adjust seasoning. Serve immediately in chilled bowls.

2 poblano chilies (roasted, peeled, seeded and julienned)
1 medium sweet onion
8 cups cubed seedless watermelon
4 oz crumbled goat cheese
1 oz fresh squeezed lime juice
2 oz extra virgin olive oil
2 tsp black sesame seeds
salt and pepper to taste

Broiled Monterey Bay Salmon With Dungeness Crab Meat Stuffed Artichoke

The Fish Hopper Restaurant, Monterey

6-8 oz fresh salmon
1 cooked artichoke heart bottom
2 oz crab cake mixture ⁎
4 tsp fresh lemon juice
1 small sliced shallot
1/8 tsp salt
1 pinch of freshly ground pepper
2 oz butter
1 diced fresh tomato
1/2 Lb fresh spinach

Mix together all crab cake ingredients, add black pepper as needed.

In a pan combine olive oil, some salt and pepper and then brush spiced oil into the fish. Cook the salmon on a grill over medium heat until done. Stuff the artichoke heart with the crab cake mixture. Cook in the oven until the crab is golden brown, about 15 minutes.

Sauce: In a hot pan put shallot, lemon juice and diced tomato until it gets warm. Take the pan off the heat; add the butter and the fresh basil. Stir well until the butter is melted; add salt and pepper for taste. For wilted spinach, heat some water in a pot and add the fresh spinach. Cook for 20 seconds. Put the fish over the spinach. Top it with stuffed artichoke heart. Finish plate by topping with the tomato basil sauce.

Crab Cake Mixture
2 oz Dungeness crab meat
1 pinch of panko bread crumbs
1 pinch of chopped parsley
2 tsp cream or mayonnaise
1 fresh egg

Blackened Louisiana Catfish With Sweet Corn Succatash

Eastside West, San Francisco
Executive Chef Scott Dammann

Cajun aoli: Combine yolks, scallion, spices and juice in food processor. With processor on slowly add oil to form an emulsion. Cool.

Dust catfish with Cajun spice. Heat skillet to smoking point put a Tbs of oil then blacken the fish on both sides, about 4 minutes. Heat saute pan with a bit of olive oil and saute onions, peppers, green tomatoes, black-eyed peas, corn, garlic, and thyme. Deglaze with Jack Daniels. Add molasses, chicken stock and reduce a bit. Finish with a dollop of butter, salt and pepper to taste and then quickly throw in the cherry tomatoes get them hot and put all on a plate. Add the blackened catfish on top, then the Cajun aoli on top of the fish. Serve with a lemon wedge.

4 filets of catfish

Succatash
2 oz red onion, medium dice
2 oz green tomatoes, medium dice
2 oz cherry tomatoes, cut in half
2 oz corn
6 oz black-eyed peas
2 oz Jack Daniels
1/4 cup chicken stock
2 tsp butter

Cajun Aoli
1 bunch scallions
4 cups olive oil
4 egg yolks
4 tsp Cajun spice
1 tsp ancho pepper powder
2 Tbs lemon juice

Sizzling Garlic Crab

Dante's Seafood Grill, Pier 39, San Francisco
Chef Leonel Jerez

Serves 2

In a saute pan heat 7 Tbs clarified butter over medium heat. Add steamed crab sections to the pan and saute for 1 minute. Add cracked black pepper, crushed red pepper, shallots, lemon grass, pickled ginger and cook until shallots are soft, about 3 minutes. Add sizzling sauce and cook about 2 minutes. Garnish with cilantro and green onions. Preheat a cast iron skillet over high heat for about 4 minutes. When ready, put all the ingredients in the skillet and serve.

20 oz Dungeness crab
sectioned, cracked
7 Tbs clarified butter
1 oz pickled ginger
1/2 tsp cracked black
pepper
1 oz lemon grass
1 bunch green onions
1/2 bunch cilantro
2 oz sliced shallots
6 oz sizzling sauce
Garlic bread (half
baguette)

Sizzling Sauce:
350 mil. ginger soy sauce
3 oz roasted whole garlic
1 bunch green onions
1 bunch cilantro
3 oz pickled ginger
3 oz pickled ginger juice
1 oz lemon grass
2 oz red chili paste

Glazed Walnut Prawns

The Mandarin, Ghirardelli Square, San Francisco

18 large prawns, shelled
and de-veined
2 cups of shelled walnuts
pinch of salt
1/2 cup sugar
2 tsp honey
1/4 tsp vanilla extract
1 tsp all purpose flour
2 large eggs, egg white
only
3 tsp mayonnaise
2 tsp sweetened
condensed milk
1 tsp of fresh lemon juice
1/2 tsp vinegar

Glazed walnuts: Bring a pot of water to boil, add walnuts and cook for 20 minutes. Drain and let dry. In a wok or a wide pot, bring mixture of sugar and salt to low boil, then add vanilla extract and honey. Quickly and evenly coat walnuts with mixture and spread out on baking sheets. Sprinkle with sesame seeds, and put into a 325-degree oven for 10-15 minutes to attain golden brown color. Once cooled, glazed walnuts can be enjoyed as it, or as a topping on salads or other dishes with sweet flavors. A shortcut is to buy walnuts already cooked and glazed.

For prawns: Combine mayonnaise, sweetened condensed milk, lemon juice and vinegar in a sauce pan over medium heat for one minute. Put aside to use to coat prawns.

Wash and dry prawns. Combine egg whites and flour and dip prawns into mixture. Put prawns into 375 degree fryer for 2-3 minutes until crispy. Drain prawns and quickly coat with sauce mixture. Top with glazed walnuts and the dish is ready to serve.

Open Faced Crab Ravioli with Diced Mango

The Crab House on Pier 39, San Francisco
Andrea Froncillo, Executive Chef

"Ravioli" means "pillows of pasta stuffed with filling" but this is not your typical ravioli! A moist crab filling is spooned atop a tender piece of pasta, and drizzled with a dreamy orange butter sauce and diced, sweet mango

Fill a small saucepan with 1 inch of water, a splash of olive oil and a sprinkle of salt. Bring the mixture to a boil; add the potsticker wraps or pasta squares, one at a time, for 3-4 minutes until they are soft. In another small saucepan over medium heat, melt the butter. Stir in orange zest, orange juice and heavy cream, stirring until thick and bubbly. Remove from heat. Assemble the filling by mixing together the crab meat, scallions and the orange zest, in a small saucepan. Add half of the heated sauce.

Place two steamed potstickers or pasta squares in the middle of a small serving plate. Spoon the crab mixture into the center (an ice cream scoop creates a nice rounded ball), then drizzle the creamy orange sauce over the top, zigzagging a little over the plate for visual interest. Sprinkle the diced mango over the top.

4 Asian potsticker wraps or one sheet of fresh pasta, cut into four equal squares
8 oz fresh crab meat
4 scallions (green onions), finely chopped
Grated zest of one orange

Orange-Butter Sauce:
2 Tbs butter
Zest of one orange
2 Tbs orange juice
1/4 cup heavy cream
1 ripe mango, peeled, seeded & finely chopped

Garlic Roasted Dungeness Crab

A. Sabella's Restaurant, San Francisco

Serves 4

Heat large pot of salted water to a boil. Add a whole lemon cut in halves, pickling spice, and salt. Plunge the crab into the water. Cook for 5 minutes. Remove from the water and let cool. Rub the fennel and potato with salt & olive oil and grill over mesquite or roast in oven until slightly tender. Note: Can be done well in advance. Place the butter and garlic in a sauce pot until melted, then simmer gently for 5 minutes. Clean and crack the crabs and place in a bowl along with all the other ingredients. Add a few pinches of salt and toss to coat everything well. Place in pan and roast in a 425 degree oven for 5-6 minutes until edges of crabs turn lightly golden brown. Arrange each crab and a portion of vegetables on a plate, spooning the garlic left in the pan over the top. Sprinkle with fennel fronds, pernod, and half a lemon.

4 lively 1 1/2 lb.
Dungeness crabs
4 oz raw garlic, pressed
or finely chopped
8 oz butter
2 oz olive oil
A pinch of kosher salt
1 head of grilled or
roasted fennel and a
dozen small potatoes
2 Tbs olive oil to coat
vegetables (add more if
needed)
One bunch lightly
chopped fennel fronds
2 lemons
6 oz Pernod
1 large pot of salted water

Striped Bass with Lacianado Kale, Calamari and Anchovy Rillette

Navio at The Ritz-Carlton, Half Moon Bay
Chef Peter Rudolph

Serves Four

4 filets of striped bass, cleaned and pin-boned by a butcher
2 Tbs cooking oil

Calamari and Kale
2 bunches of lacianado or blue russian kale, cleaned and picked from the stem
1 Lb cleaned calamari tubes, sliced thin
2 Tbs water
2 Tbs butter
2 Tbs olive oil

Anchovy Rillette
1 cup of white anchovies in oil
1 clove garlic, finely mashed
3 Tbs chopped parsley

Bass: Place oil in a hot saute pan and place the fish, skin-side down. Cook for 2 minutes and place in oven at 350 degrees Fahrenheit for 2 minutes. Turn the fish over and finish to desired temperature.

Calamari and Kale: Cook the kale in boiling water for about 8 minutes until tender, then dip in cold water. Dry the kale to remove excess water. Add olive oil to a hot saute pan, add the calamari and cook until color starts to emerge. Add the kale, water and butter, and cook for about 3 minutes until the water dissipates and the mixture is shiny and tasty.

Anchovy Rillette: Strain off the oil and cut the anchovies so they make little squares, heat the oil from the anchovies to 375 and cook the anchovies in it for about 1 minute. It should be rapidly boiling (similar to a deep-fry). Strain out the anchovies and place in an ice bath bain marie. Mix a Tbs of the oil back in to the anchovies. Add garlic and parsely.

On the plate place a portion of the kale calamari mix, set the fish on top and add a nice quenelle (or spoonful of garnish) of the rillette on the fish.

Seared Mahi Mahi With Orange & Fennel, Polenta & Fried Leeks

Portola Cafe at the Monterey Bay Aquarium
Executive Chef Tim Fisher

Serves 4

Season mahi with salt and pepper. Sear in hot olive oil until light brown, about 3 minutes on each side. (Mahi should be medium-rare). Set aside. Drain excess oil from pan, add shallots and saute until brown and tender. Add ginger, garlic and fennel, toss lightly. Add wine and continue cooking until fennel is tender and wine is almost completely reduced. Add orange juice, then salt & pepper to taste. When orange juice comes to a boil whip in butter, add orange segments and remove from heat.

Polenta: Bring water to a boil in heavy saucepan. Add 1/2 tsp salt, then add polenta slowly, stirring with a wire whip. Lower heat to a simmer and cook polenta until thick and shiny. Add butter, cheese, salt & pepper to taste.

Leeks: Slice leek in half lengthwise, cut into 2 inch pieces and julienne-slice. Season flour with salt and pepper; dust leek strips. Heat oil to 350 degrees Fahrenheit and fry leeks until brown and crispy. Place polenta in center of plate, arrange mahi around polenta, spoon over sauce, top with fried leeks and serve.

4 - 6 oz pieces mahi mahi filets
2 oz olive oil
2 shallots, diced
2 cloves garlic, sliced
1 Tbs fresh ginger, chopped
2 heads fennel, core removed, julienned
2 oz white wine
3 oranges, sectioned, pith removed
4 oz fresh squeezed orange juice
3 butter
Salt & pepper

Polenta
1/2 cup polenta
3 cups water
3 parmesan cheese
2 butter
Salt & pepper

Leeks
1 large leek
1 cup olive oil
1/2 cup of flour
Salt & pepper

California Dungeness Crab Chowder

Blue Mermaid Chowder House & Bar, San Francisco

Makes about 12 cups for a first course or 6-8 for a main course

Chowder: Over low heat, add smoked bacon to a 4 to 6 quart heavy pot. Slowly render the fat and then increase the heat to medium to make the bacon crisp. Remove the bacon from the pan and set aside. Leave about half the bacon fat in the pan. Add the butter, and saute the corn. After 4-6 minutes remove the corn from the pan. Add the onions, saute until translucent. Be careful not to brown, about 4-6 minutes. Add pasilla and saute an additional 4-minutes, then remove from the pan. Add celery and saute 2-3 minutes, then add garlic and continue to saute for an additional 2-3 minutes.

Add the onion, corn, pasilla and bacon to the celery. Add Old Bay, Chipotle powder, jalepeno pepper, thyme and bay leaf. Just barely cover the vegetables with crab stock and then add the diced Kennebec potatoes. Increase the heat to high and boil the potatoes vigorously for about 4 minutes. The goal is to soften the outside of the potato to help thicken the chowder, while keeping the potato al dente. Add the heavy cream and cream cheese stir for two minutes and then remove from the heat. If you need to thicken the chowder a little more smash a few of the potatoes against the side of the pot. Adjust the seasoning with salt and fresh white pepper. Remove the jalepeno pepper before serving. Place Chowder in a bowl, add 1 to 2 oz of crabmeat and garnish with cilantro pesto.

4 oz applewood smoked bacon
4 tbs of unsalted butter
1 cup corn
2 yellow onions, diced
1 pasilla chili, diced
1 jalepeno pepper, split in half, seeds removed
2 celery stalks
2 cloves of garlic, finely chopped
1 tsp old bay seasoning
1/2 tsp chipotle powder
4 sprigs thyme, stem removed leaves chopped
1 fresh bay leaf
1 quart crab stock
2 Lbs kennebec potatoes, 1/2-inch diced
1 1/2 cups heavy cream
2 oz cream cheese
1/2 tsp fresh ground white pepper
Kosher salt to taste
1 Lb fresh dungeness crab meat
1 bunch cilantro, diced and chopped
1/2 cup olive oil

Cilantro Pesto
1 bunch cilantro, washed , dried and chopped
Approximately 1/2 cup of olive oil puréed in a blender

Honey BBQ Prawns

Pier Market, Pier 39, San Francisco

To make honey BBQ sauce combine the first 10 ingredients in a mixing bowl and mix with a wire whisk until thoroughly combined. Put in refrigerator until ready to use. Peel and de-vein the shrimp. You may use whatever size shrimp you want, there is enough sauce in this recipe for 10 portions of 6 shrimp each. To prepare prawns heat a large skillet on the stove and add 2 tsp of olive oil for each serving of 6 shrimp. When skillet is hot add about 4 slices of the onions and peppers and saute for about 45 seconds to 1 minute. Add the 6 shrimp and saute for about 1-2 minutes until cooked about half-way through. Add 4 oz of sauce, 1/2 tsp of sesame seeds and 1 tsp of chopped basil and cilantro. Cook on high for another 2 minutes or so until the sauce is reduced by about 1/2 and the shrimp are cooked. Serve on a plate and garnish top with a sprinkle of sesame seeds and herbs.

Sauce Yields: 40 oz of sauce
10 portions of 6 shrimp per portion

Honey BBQ Sauce
1 Tbs chinese chili sauce (siracha rooster sauce)
1 1/4 cup honey
2 Tbs hot water
2 1/2 cup oyster sauce
1/3 cup ketchup
1 cup + 1 Tbs rice wine vinegar
1/2 cup teriyaki glaze
1/4 cup bbq sauce
2 tsp granulated sugar
2 Tbs garlic fresh chopped

1 each yellow onion, julienned
1 each green bell pepper, julienned
60 each 21/25 count shrimp (prawns)
Cilantro fresh chopped
Basil fresh chopped
Sesame seeds
Olive oil

Fried Monterey Bay Calamari

Passionfish, Pacific Grove
Chef Ted Walter

It is important when using this simple preparation that the freshest squid is used. Frozen product may seem flat and greasy. Quick frying and proper flouring is also essential.

To prepare: Clean squid. Slice remaining tubes of squid into three pieces. Coat the squid thoroughly in flour. Shake off excess flour. Heat oil to 350 degrees Fahrenheit. Fry squid in small batches for 40-60 seconds. Hint: The squid starts to become firm as the sizzling sound decreases. Place on towels to remove excess oil. Plate the squid on a large serving platter. Place the lemon juice, salt and pepper in three separate dishes. Instruct diners to dip each piece first in the lemon juice, then salt and pepper, and enjoy.

Serves 4-6

4 lbs fresh squid
2 cups flour
2 cups vegetable oil
2 lemons, juice only
Sea salt
Black pepper, fresh,
coarsely ground

Marinated Swordfish

Neptune's Palace, Pier 39, San Francisco
Chef Al Payton

Marinade swordfish filets for three hours in olive oil, 3 diced roasted garlic cloves, cilantro, lemon pepper and paprika. Cook at 350 degrees Fahrenheit for 8-10 minutes until done.

To make tomato relish, dice 3 Roma tomatoes, 1 clove roasted garlic, 1/4 cup fresh basil, olive oil salt and white pepper to taste. Saute 4 oz of polenta, 1 Tbs of butter, the white wine and cream, then salt and white pepper to taste. Should be consistency of thick gravy.

In a separate bowl toss the red mustard greens in 3 tsp olive oil and 1 tsp balsamic vinegar. Put creamy polenta in center of a plate. Place mustard greens over polenta. Swordfish goes on top of greens and tomato relish on fish. Garnish with a cilantro sprig.

4-6 6 oz swordfish filets
4 oz polenta
6 oz red mustard greens
3 Roma tomatoes
1/4 cup of cilantro
1/4 cup basil
4 large roasted garlic cloves
1/2 cup of olive oil
1 tsp of balsamic vinegar
2 tsp paprika
1/2 oz lemon pepper
1 Tbs butter
1/2 cup white wine
2 Tbs cream or milk

Macadamia Nut Crusted Halibut Served With Mango-Papaya Relish

Old Fisherman's Grotto Restaurant, Monterey

Serves 2-4

Four 8-oz halibut steaks
2 cups of flour
4 whole eggs, whipped
2 cups ground macadamia
nuts
Vegetable oil, for frying

Mango-Papaya Relish
1 mango, diced
1 papaya, diced
1/2 red onion, diced
1 tsp jalapeno, finely diced
1 Tbs cilantro, chopped
1/4 red bell pepper, diced
1/2 lime, juice only (fresh-
not bottled)
2 Tbs sugar
1 Tbs olive oil
1 tsp salt
1 tsp pepper

Take halibut steaks, cover them with flour, dip them in a bowl of whipped eggs and roll them on a cookie sheet with ground macadamia nuts. Pan fry in vegetable oil, about three minutes per side.

Mango-Papaya Relish: Use only ripe Mango and Hawaiian Papaya. Peel and seed both. Using a stainless steel bowl, mix together the first six ingredients then add the olive oil, lime juice, sugar, salt and pepper.

Avou Fisherman's Stew

Half Moon Bay Brewing Company, Half Moon Bay

Some of the first settlers in Half Moon Bay were from Portugal, and there still is a large Portuguese contingency here on the San Mateo Coast. In honor of that, and the fact that we are directly across from Pillar Point Harbor (the hub for our local fishermen), we serve this Portuguese-influenced stew. Its name comes from our owner's grandfather. It is one of the menu items which has remained on our menu because it is so popular.

Start pasta per pasta instructions. In a 5 quart stewing pot, saute oil, white wine, salt, pepper, garlic and shellfish Add in chicken or clam broth and steam for approximately 15 minutes, until clams open. Add fish and simmer for about 5 minutes. Add chili flakes. Divide pasta into two bowls and cover with stew. Sprinkle with tomatoes, parsley, dill, basil & fennel. Garnish with cilantro.

Serves 2

24 clams (manila or covels)
12 black mussels
2 Lb assortment of sea fish of choice (swordfish, salmon, sea bass, rock cod)
8 oz clam or chicken broth
1 good sized diced tomato
1/2 cup white wine
1/2 cup sliced fennel
1 Tbs diced garlic
1 Tbs diced cilantro
1 Tbs canola oil
1 Tbs chili flakes
1 Tbs, parsley, dill & basil
1/4 tsp salt, preferably kosher
1/4 tsp ground black peppercorns
Pasta for 2 (penne, fettuccini, linguine)

Dungeness Crab Sandwich

Louie Linguini's Seafood Shack, Monterey

Mix Dungeness crab meat, mayonnaise, lemon juice and green onion together in a large bowl. Season with salt and pepper. Meanwhile, brush olive oil on pieces of sourdough bread and toast on a grill or in the oven. Scoop Dungeness crab mixture onto toasted bread. Top with provolone cheese, tomato, lettuce and additional slice of bread.

Serves 4 persons.

1 1/2 Lbs Dungeness crabmeat
4 oz mayonnaise
4 oz lemon juice
2 oz green onion
4 slices tomato
4 pieces lettuce
4 slices provolone cheese
8 slices sourdough bread
Olive oil
Salt & pepper

Fetuccine ai Frutti di Mare

Tre Fratelli

Cook pasta in salted and oiled boiling water for seven minutes. Check after 5 minutes for an al dente consistency. Drain pasta and coat with olive oil if it will sit for more than a couple of minutes to avoid sticking. In a large pan melt butter. Add olive oil and onions until onions are transparent. Add garlic, peppers, mushrooms, scallops, white fish, prawns, clams and mussels. Cook on high and toss for one or two minutes to sear. Add white wine and mix to deglaze the pan. Add Half and Half, saffron and strained pasta. Salt and pepper to taste. Mix and serve making sure the seafood stands out. Sprinkle with fresh Italian parsley.

Serves 1-2

8 oz of fresh fetuccine
1 Tbs butter
1/12 tsp olive oil
1 oz chopped onions
1/4 tsp chopped garlic
1 oz of fresh white fish, your choice
2-4 scallops or calamari
2-4 prawns
4 clams
4 mussels
2 oz of mushrooms (optional)
2 oz of red and yellow peppers
1 oz of white wine
6 oz of Half & Half
1/4 tsp of saffron threads (optional)
Salt, pepper to taste
Sprinkle with fresh oregano

Ravioli con Granchio

Cafe Pescatore, San Francisco
Chef de Cuisine Rafael Mayoral

"Alla tabella con i buoni amici e famiglia non diventate vecchi"
At the table with good friends and family you do not become old. - Italian Proverb

Pasta: Combine dry ingredients in a standard mixer with a dough hook attachment on low speed. Add oil and eggs slowly and mix for 10- 15 minutes, adding water only as needed to form an elastic dough. Wrap in plastic and let rest in the refrigerator for 30-40 minutes before using. If making and rolling the dough is more of a project than you want, wonton wrappers can be used as the pasta to be filled.

Filling: Heat a skillet over high heat and add 1 Tbs of vegetable oil and crab meat. Lower heat and sauté for 3-5 minutes, just until cooked but not dry. Cool before processing. Place cool crab meat in a food processor and pulse just to chop, do not puree it smooth. Turn crab meat into a bowl and add the rest of the ingredients and season with salt and pepper to taste. Cover and refrigerate for 30 minutes.

Assembly: Roll out pasta dough to 1/16th inch thickness either by hand or with a pasta machine and cut out 3-inch circles or squares. Paint each piece lightly with an egg wash. Place a small amount of filling in the center of the pasta, cover with another piece of dough and press to secure. Use this same procedure if using wonton sheets. Pasta is cooked when it floats to the top of the boiling water.

Sauce: In a large skillet heat 2 Tbs oil over medium heat and add leeks, asparagus and shallots and sauté until leeks are soft, 3 minutes. Add marinara sauce, cream, fish stock and basil and simmer to reduce until desired thickness is obtained, 3-5 minutes. Season with salt and pepper and toss with cooked ravioli.

Pasta
3 cups semolina
1 cup flour
5 eggs
2 Tbs oil
1 Tbs salt
1/2 cup water

Filling
2 1/2 Lbs fresh crab meat
1/4 cup chopped basil
1 Lb ricotta cheese
1 Tbs of vegetable oil
Salt and pepper to taste
1 egg (for egg wash)

Sauce: Serves 4
6 oz of fresh tomatoes diced
1 leek, julienned
1 bunch of asparagus, washed and diced
1 shallot minced
1/4 cup fresh basil chopped
1/2 cup fish stock
1 1/2 cup heavy cream
1 cup of marinara sauce
Salt and pepper to taste

Grilled Salmon With Ponzu Sauce

Shadowbrook, Capitola

1 cup orange juice
1 cup sake
1/2 cup sugar
1/2 cup soy sauce
1/2 Tbs fresh lime juice
1/4 tsp dried crushed red pepper
1/4 tsp cracked black pepper
2 tsp water
1 1/2 tsp cornstarch
Vegetable oil
Six 7-8 oz salmon fillets
1 Tbs black sesame seeds or toasted sesame seeds
6 lemon wedges

Ponzu Sauce: Combine orange juice, sake, sugar, soy sauce, lime juice and red pepper in heavy small saucepan. Bring to boil over medium-high heat, stirring until sugar dissolves. Boil until mixture is reduced to 1 1/3 cups, about 5 minutes. Combine 2 teaspoons water and cornstarch in small bowl, stirring until cornstarch dissolves. Add cornstarch mixture to ponzu sauce and boil until sauce thickens and is clear, stirring frequently, about 1 minute. (Ponzu sauce can be prepared up to 1 day ahead of time. Cover and refrigerate. Ponzu also available at Japanese markets and natural food stores and in the Asian foods section of some supermarkets)

Prepare barbecue (medium-high heat). Brush grill with vegetable oil. Brush each salmon fillet with 1 Tbs ponzu sauce. Grill salmon skin side up, 3 minutes. Turn salmon fillets and brush each with another 1 Tbs ponzu sauce. Grill until salmon is just cooked through, about 5 minutes. Transfer one salmon fillet to each of 6 plates. Sprinkle with sesame seeds; garnish with lemon wedges and serve.

Skyy Melon Martini

Served up in a martini glass with melon ball garnish

2 oz Chilled SKYY Melon
A splash of lemon-lime soda

Straight-Up Skyy

S hake SKYY with ice, strain into a chilled martini glass. Simply garnish with two olives on a pick.

2 oz SKYY Vodka
2 olives

RESOURCES

Chocolate & Cocoa

Ghirardelli Chocolate Shop & Caffe
900 North Point Street, Box 142
West Plaza of Ghirardelli Square
San Francisco
415-474-1414

Guittard Chocolate Company
10 Guittard Road
Burlingame
800-468-2462

Quetzal
1234 Polk
San Francisco
415-673-4181

Scharffen Berger Chocolate Maker
914 Heinz Avenue
Berkeley
800-930-4528

XOX Truffles
754 Columbus Avenue
San Francisco
415-421-4814

Decor, Design & Supplies

ARTwork SF
www.artworksf.com
415-673-3080
(Art purchases, rentals, commissions)

Cafe Society
2 Henry Adams Street #360
San Francisco
415-487-2333 x115
www.cafesocietystore.com
(Cafe Decor & Antiques)

Tinhorn Press/Gallery
511 Laguna Street
San Francisco
415-621-1292
(Combination gallery and working printshop)

Music

Putumayo World Music
324 Lafayette Street, 7th Floor
New York, NY
1-888 PUTUMAYO (788-8629)
1-800-995-9588 ext. 226 (for Cafes & Retailers)

Cafe del Mar, Version 7
MCA Records
(Various Outlets)

Tours

Barbary Coast Trail
San Francisco Museum & Historical Society
San Francisco
415-454-2355

Franciscan Lines/Coach USA
Pier 43 1/2
San Francisco
415-434-8687
415-642-9400

Walking Tours San Francisco
925 Sutter Street, Suite 101
San Francisco
415-931-4021
Mangia! North Beach Tour with GraceAnn Walden
415-397-8530
gaw@sbcglobal.net

Syrups

Torani Italian Syrups
Torre R & Co.
233 E. Harris Avenue
South San Francisco
800-775-1925

Cheese

Cowgirl Creamery
P.O. Box 594
80 Fourth Street
Point Reyes Station
415-663-9335

Cowgirl Creamery
The Ferry Building Marketplace
One Ferry Building, Marketplace Shop #17
San Francisco
415-362-9354

Seafood, Meat and Poultry

Golden Gate Meat Company
@ The Ferry Building Marketplace
One Ferry Building, Shop 13
San Francisco
415-983-7800

GGMC Corporate Headquarters
550 Seventh Street
San Francisco
415-861-3800

Hog Island Oysters
PO Box 829
Marshall
415-663-9218

Torani

Torani flavored syrups are a part of San Francisco's Italian heritage. In 1925, husband and wife team Rinaldo and Ezilda Torre began blending Italian syrups from heirloom recipes that Rinaldo had brought from Lucca, Italy. The pair soon perfected five flavors - Anisette, Grenadine, Lemon, Orgeat (almond) and Tamarindo - and shared them with their neighbors throughout North Beach, San Francisco's flourishing Italian community. Mixed with soda water, the syrups were instantly a local favorite, and café & bar owners in America were introduced to the "Italian Soda." The R. Torre & Company was born, and a line of authentic Italian syrups emerged, under the brand name "Torani."

Over the next sixty years, Torani grew into a nationally recognized brand. Then, in the 1980's, coffee industry veteran "Brandy" Brandenburger noticed the brightly colored Torani bottles while visiting San Francisco's landmark café, Caffé Trieste. Experimenting with various blends, he added a shot of Torani to an espresso drink, hoping the flavor might lend a new appeal to the traditional beverage. With this mixture Brandenburger created and introduced the novel concept of the flavored caffe latte. Soon coffee lovers everywhere were requesting Torani-flavored espresso drinks and a new American classic was born. The rest is history. For decades,

Torani's red, gold and blue labels have been a part of the cafe lifestyle. Much has changed over the years, but Torani is still family-owned and -operated in South San Francisco, not far from its North Beach origins. Torani now exports over 70 syrup flavors across the country and around the world and continues to offer new ways to add flavor and originality to beverages and culinary pursuits.

Consumers can purchase Torani at select grocery stores, specialty retailers and through online distributors. Restaurants, bars and cafes can purchase Torani products through their distributor or by contacting Torani directly for more information. Go to www.torani.com, or call 800-775-1925.

Hog Island Oyster Company
PO Box 829
Marshall

Hog Island Oyster Company
The Ferry Building Marketplace
One Ferry Building, Marketplace Shop #11-1
San Francisco
415-391-7117

San Francisco Fish Company
1 Ferry Building Suite 31
San Francisco
415-399-1111

Architects

BAR Architects
1660 Bush St.
San Francisco
415 441-4771

C. David Robinson
250 Sutter Street, Suite 600
San Francisco
415-291-8680

Heller·Manus Inc.
dba Heller·Manus Architects
221 Main Street, Suite 940
San Francisco
415.247.1100

LOCUS Architecture West
450 Geary St., 5th Flr.
San Francisco
415-474 - 5345

Museums

San Francisco Maritime NHP
Building E, Fort Mason Center
San Francisco
415-561-7006

Maritime Park Association
P.O. Box 470310
San Francisco
415-561-6662

The San Francisco Maritime Museum
900 Beach Street
San Francisco

Beach Chalet Visitors Center
1000 Great Highway
San Francisco

Visitors to the Park Chalet in San Francisco

South San Francisco, Photo by Ben Swire

INDEX